ISLAND *Cycling*

A Cycle Camper's Guide
to Vancouver Island

DAVID PAYNE

ORCA BOOK PUBLISHERS

The information in this book is accurate and complete to the best of our knowledge. The author and publisher disclaim any liability in connection with the use of this information.

Canadian Cataloguing in Publication Data
Payne, David J. (David John), 1946–
Island cycling

Includes bibliographical references and index.
ISBN 1-55143-082-7

1. Bicycle touring—British Columbia—Vancouver Island—Guidebooks.
2. Vancouver Island (B.C.)—Guidebooks. I. Title.
GV1046.C32V35 1996 796.6'4'097112 C95–911167–0

Cover design: Christine Toller
Cover photograph: Gary Green
Interior photographs: Alison Payne
Maps: Lara Payne
Editor: Andrew Wooldridge
Printed and bound in Canada

Orca Book Publishers
PO Box 5626, Station B
Victoria, BC V8R 6S4
Canada

Orca Book Publishers
PO Box 468
Custer, WA 98240-0468
USA

10 9 8 7 6 5 4 3 2 1

To Judy and Terry.
Our shared experiences have brought
both joy and heartache.
And to Alison, whom I love.

R

Table of Contents

Foreword vii
Summary of Routes ix
About This Book 1

Part 1 — An Introduction to Cycle Touring on the Island

The Island 3
Equipment: Bicycle & Accessories 12
Equipment: Camping Gear 24
Equipment: Pubs 35
Campgrounds 38

Part 2 — Routes

Methodology 42
Saanich Peninsula 44
Greater Victoria 52
Salt Spring Island 61
The Cowichan Valley Wine Road 69
Cowichan Lake 77
North Cowichan 87
Nanaimo 96
Nanaimo/Coombs/Port Alberni 107
Ucluelet/Tofino via Alberni Inlet 116
Comox Valley 123
Denman and Hornby Islands 131
Cumberland/Courtenay/Comox 138
Comox Valley/Campbell River 147
Campbell River/Sayward/Woss Camp 154
Sointula/Alert Bay 161
Telegraph Cove/Port McNeill/Port Hardy 167
Appendices
I Metric Conversion Table 175
II Distance Chart 175
III Travel Infocentres 176
Bibliography 178
Index 179

Foreword

I am a passionate man. Not that I have a lot of passions, but those that I have I hold, well ... passionately. This book is about some of my main loves.

As a kid, I rode my bike long after it was considered cool to do so. "J.C. Higgins" took me to school, helped with my paper and drugstore routes, participated in boyhood adventures, and carried me to my first real job. As an adult, cycling has introduced me to friendships, experiences and places without which I would be a much different person.

Camping to me has always been a kind of wonderful game. Its challenge is comfort — being warm, dry and adequately fed. Winning requires successful planning, practical equipment, and effective technique. It's a diversion and release. And there's nothing like a few days of living outside to put life back into perspective.

On Vancouver Island we are fortunate to have a lot of pubs, magically distributed at twenty- to thirty-kilometre intervals along many of the main and secondary roads. Each has its own character, all serve great beer, and most feature pretty good grub. They are justifiable periodic diversions for the sweaty, tired cyclist who loves suds and gets too much healthy food at home.

Pleasure is best with company. Even better if that company includes a conjugal other to share experiences and assist with getting to bed on time. In my case, this is my wife of twenty-six years, a tremendously fit lady who has always asserted I am blessed with excess testosterone. ("Blessed" is my word.)

For years writing has been part of how I make a living. Mostly stuffy, precise and technical, and of interest to a limited readership: my clients — who thankfully are willing to pay me for it. This is a first attempt at writing for fun, combining pursuit of my passions with a facility for language and a sense of humour.

Hopefully I've been able to share this with the reader.

Writing a book, even a small book, is a big job, which I could not have accomplished alone. At the risk of omitting some important contributors, I wish to acknowledge those who assisted me by providing the necessary facts, and the skills with which to write about them. At the very beginning is my mother, Irene Payne, who at our dining room table in England gave me a pre-school head start with reading and writing. And after innumerable attempts finally convinced me that there was no "b" in "plum."

Thank you to Dr. Ferguson, my high school English teacher who imprinted in me the notion that "concise speech reflects concise thought." Ditto Mr. Young, my Latin teacher. And to Mr. Kellway, who had the compassion to help an average student, struggling to qualify for university, to see beyond the mechanics of language to its imagery.

I am grateful to my friends and associates in the Island Canada Employment Centres for their invaluable research assistance on the various Island communities. Thanks to the many individuals who gave the time to provide the anecdotes that made this book possible. And to Bob Tyrrell, my editor and publisher, who took a chance with a fledgling author.

Over the years Alison, David Moddle, Tom Brown, Bill Scott, Judy Napper and Terry Napper have ridden with me to share adventures, and sometimes create them. Some of these pals also come with supplementary benefits. David Moddle, gentleman and friend, is the best camper I know. Tom Brown ensures that my computing problems are only temporary. And an association with Bill Scott provides the continuing comfort of knowing at least one person who is in worse shape than I.

I am indebted to Alison for her editing and photography, and patience in not reminding me too often while this book was being written that there was no money coming in. To Cindy Bertram, my business partner, who tolerated my distractions from business. Once more to Tom Brown, whose wit nurtures mine. To Judy Napper for shaking loose in me the desire to write. And my daughter Lara, whose response when I told her that I would have liked to be a writer was "So why don't you?".

Finally, thank you to the anonymous wood boat builder who reportedly coined the phrase "God lives in the details."

David J. Payne
Nanaimo, BC, 1996

Summary of Routes

Main Route	Side Route(s)	Distance	Type	Page
Saanich Peninsula		50 km*	Circuit	44
	San Juan Islands	50-65 km	Circuit(s)	50
	Saanich Peninsula Backroads	Various**	Various**	51
Greater Victoria		55 km	Linear	52
	Galloping Goose Regional Trail	47 km	Linear	60
Salt Spring Island		55 km	Circuit	61
	Mount Maxwell Provincial Park	9 km	Linear	67
	The North Circuit	25 km	Circuit	68
Cowichan Valley Wine Road		76 km	Circuit	69
	Malahat Drive/Shawnigan Lake	40 km	Circuit	76
Cowichan Lake				
Cowichan River railway beds		42 km	Circuit	81
Port Renfrew via the Logging Roads		108 km	Circuit	83
Around the lake		76 km	Circuit	86
North Cowichan		63 km	Circuit	87
Nanaimo		46 km	Circuit	96
	Gabriola Island	33 km	Circuit	104
	Yellow Point	57 km	Circuit	105
	Nanaimo Lakes	61 km	Circuit	106
Nanaimo/Coombs/Port Alberni		77 km	Linear	107
	Northwest Bay logging roads	Various	Various	112
	The Log Train Trail	43 km	Circuit	114
Ucluelet/Tofino via Alberni Inlet		45 km	Linear	116
Comox Valley		68 km	Linear	123
	Horne Lake	Various	Various	129
Denman and Hornby Islands		47 km	Circuit	131
	Mount Geoffrey	10-15 km	Circuit	137
Cumberland/Courtenay/Comox		60 km	Circuit	138
	Mount Washington	27 km	Linear	144
	Powell River and Texada Island	Various	Various	145
Comox Valley/Campbell River		53 km	Linear	147
	John Hart Dam	27 km	Circuit	152
	Quadra Island	25 km	Circuit	152
Campbell River/Sayward/Woss Camp		135 km	Linear	154
Sointula/Alert Bay		30 km	Circuit	161
Telegraph Cove/Port McNeill/Port Hardy		58 km	Linear	167

* 1 kilometer = 0.6 miles
** distance and type depend on the traveller's choice of route

About This Book

This book was inspired by a planned trip to Ireland. My wife, Alison, and I had just survived a particularly unpleasant period that had culminated in a short separation. In the soul searching that preceded our reunion we each came to recognize that for some time we had stopped communicating. In the past we had shared our dreams and chased them together. Then we had started pursuing individual agendas and neglecting each other.

A trip to Ireland would be a large step toward reconciliation. Alison had always wanted to go there, and I had heard it was a cyclist's dream. The advance research, preparation and physical training (we planned to cycle all Ireland in one month) would offer a chance to enjoy each other's company while pursuing a common goal.

The research appeared to be the easy part. Ireland's been around for a few thousand years, and bikes for over a hundred. And if the scores of bikes we see each year with camping gear attached are an indication, cycle touring combined with tenting is a huge pastime. Surely somebody would have documented the unique skills and equipment needed to pursue this pastime successfully. Wrong!

While there is ample documentation of cycle touring in Ireland, and on Vancouver Island for that matter, it seems to have been prepared by folks with more money than us. They didn't find it necessary to camp. Or if they did, felt that the knowledge and experiences associated with cycle camping were of no interest to the reader. For example, we were unable to ascertain from any references whether there was fuel available in Ireland for our naphtha-burning cook stove.

We also noted that the prevailing format was that of a travelogue, written by individuals more obsessed with documentation than having fun. Teacher (or student, or professor) visits briefly, then returns during summer to cycle and record every rock, church, hill and turn on the route.

The reader may have observed by now that Ireland to Vancouver Island is a fair leap. So here's the connection. We realized that the information we lacked for Ireland was also largely unavailable for our own Vancouver Island. And since we had to train and prepare for the Ireland trip, why not accomplish these by researching, on our bikes, precisely the information we would like to have seen available about Ireland? Besides, the millions in publisher's royalties would pay for the Ireland trip. And we'd have enough money that we wouldn't have to stay in a tent.

In the past few years I have camped and cycled thousands of kilometres on Vancouver Island. This book retraces some old routes and adds new ones. It is not a travelogue — that information has been more ably completed by others. Rather it is a guide to some favourite routes.

Some routes are circular and represent a comfortable day's travel with the same start and end points. Others are linear, and frequently but not always connect to another route. Each day's travel offers a watering hole or two, the occasional anecdote, and a decent spot to pitch a tent at day's end. I have included a general overview of the terrain the cyclist can expect to encounter, the services available, and some background to the communities and other sights. The latter are by no means all-inclusive. A visitor to the Island quickly learns there is a richness of human and natural history here to fill volumes.

My book is intended for both the avid and casual cycling camper, as well as the armchair traveller who just enjoys a good read.

The Island

To those of us who live here, Vancouver Island is simply "the Island." Other Canadians live on "the mainland." "Mainland" doesn't warrant a capital "M" because mainlanders haven't yet figured out that the only place to live in Canada is the Island.

The Island is about the size of an average European country — 3,175,000 hectares accommodated in 450 km of length. It features balmy weather (by Canadian standards), fantastic scenery, clean air and water, and a host of year-round activities. It is still mostly a wilderness of mountains and forests. We like to brag that in the winter you can go skiing in the morning and salmon fishing in the afternoon. In the summer there are so many options available to the users of private and public facilities that operators sometimes have a tough time making a go of it. People of all ages retire here by the thousands.

Since the Island is also dead centre in the resource and environment controversies of the nineties, people also go broke and get unemployed here by the thousands. We moved here in 1987 from Toronto, I having decided to abandon Bay Street. In retrospect I'm sure I'm far better off being broke in balmy weather and fantastic scenery than working in that silly old affluent smog of T.O.

To the cyclist the Island is a dream. It offers urban, rural and wilderness opportunities for all levels of fitness and expertise. The adventurer can plan routes that are mostly flat, with a gas station, a McDonald's, or a pub only a few minutes away. Alternatively, we have pedalled on logging roads in the mountains where a broken leg to the lone cyclist could mean never having to make another mortgage payment.

The first-time cyclist on the Island will immediately be aware of its beauty and recreational potential. Less apparent will be that it is hilly and occasionally rainy, and that the roads are sometimes a tad unsafe. Knowing this will assist the cycling camper in planning the best routes and choosing the right equipment.

This book also includes reference to the Gulf Islands, an extensive archipelago on our side of Georgia Strait. We have come to regard these as a personal playground, by virtue of their proximity and ease of access by ferry.

Each possesses the character and amenities of the Island, supplemented by its own uniqueness which can best be experienced by visiting.

Hills

Canada's west coast is known for its mountains, and these extend throughout the Island. Most of the Island's cities and towns, and the roads that service them, are squeezed between its eastern shoreline and interior mountains. The terrain can vary from seashore flat, to rolling hills, to 5 percent, or worse, grades that extend for kilometres. Several years ago north of Sayward we spent most of one day ascending hills. It is unlikely that the cyclist travelling for a whole day will not encounter at least one major grade.

Although we've travelled the Island on ten-speed touring cycles, the best bikes for this terrain are twenty-one-speed mountain bikes or hybrids. In addition to offering the extra comfort associated with a larger selection of gears, they are more ruggedly constructed to handle the torque needed to travel uphill under load.

Rain

Paradise needs some rain. The old-growth forests here are several hundred metres high and they drink a lot of water. Nature accommodates us by raining mostly between October and March, when few visitors are around to notice. In the other months it rains much less, and is particularly sunny in the second half of summer and early fall. However, regardless of the season, any extended visit is likely to encounter some rain, which can vary from foggy drizzle to a major downpour.

My experience has been that rain is much harder on bikes than it is on people. Water thrown up from the road carries grit that rapidly wears down brake pads, rims and bearings. The rear derailleur on my Shimano XT-equipped Giant, my all-time-favourite cycle and a pal for the past three years, has the annoying idiosyncrasy of hopping between gears as soon as it starts to rain.

Keeping myself dry in the rain is not an issue, because I perspire a fair amount. In fact I sweat buckets — so many buckets that it is irrelevant whether the moisture on my body is generated internally or deposited by Mother Nature. However, a couple of close encounters with hypothermia have taught me that it's a damn good idea to have dry, warm clothing handy when the day's riding is over.

Roads

No description of the Island would be complete without some commentary on the roads, not that they're bad by South American standards. A negative consequence of the rapid population growth here has been the inability of the highway infrastructure to keep pace. To its credit, the Ministry of Highways recognizes this and a massive upgrading project is currently underway. So some of the following narrative may soon be obsolete.

Aside from the streets in the cities and towns, which are typically well-paved, well-lit and safe, there are three types of road on the Island — the Island Highway, secondary roads and logging roads.

The Island Highway is the main route linking Island points north and south. It includes the first leg of the Trans-Canada Highway, which runs from Victoria to Nanaimo (before crossing to the mainland by ferry). The Island Highway continues up the east coast to Port Hardy, with an intersecting spur just north of Nanaimo offering access to Port Alberni and points west. Because the Island Highway is the main, and frequently only, connector, between Island communities, it is busy year-round with cars, trucks and buses. In the summer this already considerable traffic is augmented by hundreds of thousands of holiday visitors. For about four months the Island Highway is an only-intermittently broken line of vehicles from Campbell River to Victoria. Many of these are recreational vehicles driven by elderly retirees and occasional renters who mostly haven't a clue how to keep these big suckers between the lines. Cyclists are objects to avoid, where possible.

The wary rider should also know that at the moment the Island Highway is frequently a two-lane affair, although the paved shoulders are reasonably wide and the grades moderate. The Island Highway Project, which is linking communities up the Island with a modified island route, will be largely complete by 1999. It promises to allevite east-coast congestion and could make north-south cycling safer and more pleasant.

Secondary roads are mostly feeder routes into the Island Highway, although they occasionally provide a substitute route. Typically they are all paved, but narrower, windier and more hilly, and have limited or no paved shoulders.

We take secondary roads whenever possible. They have less traffic, more interesting scenery, and a generally more relaxed pace. Most of the tours in this book utilize secondary roads.

The logging roads traverse those parts of the Island not serviced by the paved roads, which is to say most of it. They are the primary medium by which the forest harvest is brought to market. All are gravel surfaced and many are well maintained. It is on the logging roads that one is most likely to glimpse deer and bears, which abound here. Once, while cycling on a logging road near Port Renfrew, we were stopped by an oncoming trucker and warned that he had seen bears ahead. I was taught that when bears are around, it's smart to make noise. As we sang and clanged our way along the next few kilometres and saw no bears, I had a vision of that driver telling his story later in the pub to his buddies. "Met a couple of cyclists in those funny outfits on the main line. Jes' for fun told 'em I'd seen some bears up ahead. Shoulda seen their faces! Bet those poor slickers sang all the way to Mesachie Corners." Neat trick. Wish I'd thought of it myself. There are also cougar and some elk herds. I saw an elk for the first time while researching this book. I have never seen a cougar.

The properly equipped cyclist who doesn't mind a little logging truck dust can access some extraordinary wilderness — usually lakeshore — campsites from the logging roads.

A final comment is desirable regarding the relationship between Island drivers and cyclists. Research indicates that a growing number of our drivers originated in large urban areas, presumably where sound driving skills, including courtesy and adherence to the rules of the road, are survival skills. Occasionally there is little evidence of this. Perhaps it is the frustration of dealing with an overburdened infrastructure, or unfamiliarity with encountering the increasingly large numbers of cyclists, or the behaviour of cyclists themselves (my wife made me put that one in). In any event we have discerned no serious attempts to educate either drivers or cyclists.

My friend Judy, a long-time cycling companion, swears by the middle-finger salute. Unfortunately that makes me the alternate target of the infuriated trucker too genteel to want to beat the snot out of a woman.

The People

The Island's population of about 600,000, is concentrated on its southeast coast.

In its early history the Island was populated entirely by those who derived their existence from its abundant land and sea resources. Aboriginals, who currently number only a small fraction of their early population, prospered here for centuries. Then a hundred and fifty years ago the Europeans came here to fish, hunt, log and mine. During this period they also introduced diseases, particularly small pox, to which the natives had no immunity. Over time the aboriginals who did not perish were confined to reserves, where for the most part, they remain — frequently without work, in return for relinquishing the lands from which they derived their livelihood.

There are many reserves on the Island, located in urban, rural and wilderness areas. Some courageous and dignified individuals are working to restore their once proud cultures. This book was never intended to make a social statement. However, I would have been remiss in trivializing the status of the native population.

Non-native society for its part has undergone a radical, although more subtle transition. While fishing, logging and mining continue to be notable economic engines, their importance and the jobs they create have been eroded by diminishing resources, technological impact and environmental concerns. The economy is now driven significantly by those who come here to retire, visit, play or telecommute. Employment opportunities are in the areas of tourism, hospitality, recreation, construction and information management. Our resultant labour force is a potpourri of highly skilled, and those busy acquiring new skills. Most are working, or don't need to.

To many that I have met, the Island represents an opportunity for change and personal renewal. For retirees, many of whom are only in their fifties, the weather, scenery and recreational opportunities represent an ideal venue. For those of us poor stiffs who still have to work, frequently assisted by technology and its ability to connect us to remote markets, the time we used to spend commuting can now be utilized to play. Most people I meet have come here from another part of Canada, having moved here "for the lifestyle."

When we first considered relocating here we made a quick advance trip to research our opportunities. The unemployment rate at the time was about 20 percent. One night at dinner, we asked our server, an obviously bright young man if this bothered him. His response: "80 percent of us are working!"

In my real job I study people as statistics, a vocation which suits my moderately anti-social nature. However, for some reason wearing lycra cycling pants and drinking beer makes me companionable, and interested in the individuals I meet, many of whom contributed to the writing of this book.

Economy

Although not marked on any map of the Island, those of us living here understand it to be divided geographically and economically into three regions, south, central and north. A broad overview of each of these follows. Many will be addressed in greater detail as this book progresses.

The south Island is the area south of the Malahat, a mountainous ridge about thirty kilometres north of Victoria which separates the southern part of the Island from the rest. The Malahat is traversed mainly by a single paved route, the Island Highway, which offers a thrilling challenge to the cyclist. The south Island has the largest population concentration on the Island, about 350,000, which includes inhabitants of Victoria, a beautiful city with a distinctly British flavour, and its outlying suburbs. Victoria is BC's provincial capital, and as such houses the legislature, many of the province's bureaucrats, and several Crown Corporations. The region itself is sufficiently large to support a broad commercial, agricultural and industrial base, much of which is becoming increasingly high tech.

Those of us who don't live in the south consider it to be culturally distinct — urbane and faster paced. People there frequently dress in suits and ties, apparel which the rest of us reserve mainly for funerals.

The central Island is bounded by the Malahat to the south and Campbell River to the north, encompassing a population of about 200,000 in several cities and towns, the largest of which is Nanaimo. This area enjoys a rich and colourful resource-based history. It was home to several significant commercial and sport fisheries, whaling grounds, mining, and agriculture, and until the early 1900s a world-renowned coal mining centre

While natural resources, particularly the forests and fishery, still offer a substantial economic base, they are shrinking. But the area continues to prosper. Each year it attracts tens of thousands of tourists, and since the mid-eighties has become a popular retirement destination.

Resources, particularly logging and fishing, are the economic kings of the north Island, the remaining area north of Campbell River. This is still mostly wilderness populated by the occasional small community, of which Port Hardy is by far the largest with a population of five thousand. These communities usually started life as a sheltered harbour in which to anchor a fish boat, or load logs.

The cyclist is conscious of abrupt change when heading north on the Highway from Campbell River. Traffic reduces to a trickle — even on busy weekends — there are few businesses or residences, and the road turns inland across mountains with spectacular views of nothing but forest. The area has recently become a mecca for the visitor who enjoys the outdoors. It is one of my favourite places in Canada to visit, and still retains the cultural charm, typical to remote areas, that values hospitality.

Miscellaneous Considerations

BC Ferries

With 40 ships plying 24 coastal routes, the BC Ferries fleet is larger than most navies. The service began in 1960 with two ships connecting Victoria and Vancouver. The fleet presently transports about 8 million vehicles and 24 million passengers annually, most of these between the mainland, Vancouver Island and the Gulf Islands.

While the Island is served by several regional airlines, by far the most common and practical way to arrive is by ferry. An extensive ferry network also services the Gulf Islands. Ferry schedules are available at all tourist information centres, and on the ferries themselves. Except during the busiest of long weekends, ferries are remarkably punctual.

Cyclists usually enjoy the same first-on and first-off status as foot passengers, so it's a good idea to be at the terminal a few minutes ahead of scheduled departure time. Upon disembarking the rider will nearly always encounter a steep hill. Although first off, it's a good idea to wait at the side of road until disembarking vehicles have passed. This avoids inhaling their exhaust, and the lack of concern for cyclists by motorists impatient to reach their destinations.

BC Ferries Corporation, a Crown company, only recently began charging for bicycles. Riders once paid just the foot passenger fare. However the ever vigilant BC government quickly recognized the potential of a growing sport to add to our already infamous taxes. There is now a separate charge for bicycles, in return for which the cyclist is given a spot on the lowest deck, often jammed between a semi-trailer and the wall, and sometimes a piece of string with which to secure the bike.

A ride on a BC ferry is an experience of which the Corporation is justifiably proud. Seating is plentiful and comfortable, BC coastal scenery is always worth viewing, and the quality of food at least equals what I can create at a campsite.

The metric system (for the information of out-of-Canada visitors)

A couple of decades ago our federal government determined to abolish the imperial measurement system, a legacy of our British founders, in favour of metric. The wisdom of that time held that since most of the rest of the world was metric, by converting to it we would benefit from increased international trade. Unfortunately this ignored the United States, also on the imperial system, and our neighbour and largest trading partner. The USA was too prudent to expose either its citizens or its economy to the trauma of metrication.

Those of us of a certain age, about forty and over, learned the British system as children, in the British way — by countless hours of repetition and memorization. Imperial measures are permanently and unalterably embedded in our psyches. Because of this and our country's considerable cultural and economic interaction with the United States, we have had to develop a sort of dichotomous thought process. For example, we buy our plywood in 8' x 4' sheets, play our football on a 110 yard field, but are assessed in kilometres per hour for our speeding tickets. We need to own two sets of socket wrenches, one metric and the other imperial. And the correct response to a query on the distance to the nearest supermarket will frequently be governed by the age or nationality of the asker — about a mile for middle aged and older or American, otherwise 1.5 km.

Strangely enough a pint of beer is still a pint of beer. I've never heard it ordered by the liter. Maybe it tastes different that way.

While this book mostly utilizes metric measurement; for those unfamiliar or uncomfortable with it, a conversion table is included as an appendix.

Personal safety

Because I frequently travel alone, I am asked about any concerns I might have about my personal safety. I am comfortable in my own company, and because I'm male and big, I probably don't present a desirable target to potential human predators. In thousands of kilometres travelled I can recount not a single incidence of either myself or my companions being threatened — other than by erratic motorists, a circumstance I ascribe to incompetence rather than malice.

I have met a few women who were cycling alone. Occasionally they have tales of fear — usually short-term harassment by males with libidos as large as their pick-up trucks. One young woman, a graduate student who had cycled alone here from Idaho, carries pepper spray. She has never had to use it, but volunteered that it contributes greatly to her peace of mind.

The Island's urban and rural areas are no more or less safe than other places in Canada. The traveller is advised to take the same precautions as in any other part of this country, and stay within his/her own comfort range.

Travel Infocentres

Most Island communities have a tourist information office, to which one is directed by roadside signs erected on major access routes. These are staffed by knowledgeable individuals, frequently volunteers, who have a genuine interest in assisting travellers and promoting their communities.

They are stocked with books and brochures on local and Island-wide sights, facilities and historical details, most of which are free.

I recommend to the Island visitor:

- *Provincial Parks of Vancouver Island*
- *British Columbia Road Map and Parks Guide*
- *Parks of Vancouver Island*
- *Where — Vancouver Island*
- *British Columbia First Nations Guide*
- *Super, Natural Islands*
- *British Columbia Super Camping*
- A Free *Visitors Guide* to Northern Vancouver Island

These are all available without charge and are excellent references.

The forestry industry has also seen a need to establish information centres in some communities. Forestry centres offer the visitor a range of handouts and exhibits relevant to plants and animals, silviculture practices, and forest-related social and ecological issues.

Our forests support thousands of jobs and are a huge contributor to the local and national economies. But the industry is threatened. Forest practices have been under intense scrutiny and criticism, sometimes international. Much of this has been negative, and deservedly so. A clear-cut is more than an ugly indiscretion, it affronts nature. However in some instances the industry is condemned for practices that have already been, or are being corrected.

The centres are worth visiting for their scientific information, as well as to acquire other perspectives on the forest-resource controversy. Of particular interest to the cycling camper are their maps, also free, which designate the logging roads and campsites in reliable detail, a must for anyone opting to travel in these areas.

Equipment: Bicycle & Accessories

There are already many good books on the basic specifications, construction, selection and care of bicycles, some of which are included in the bibliography. Consequently I will address the basics only briefly, focusing instead on the equipment modifications and accessories which facilitate cycle camping.

For purposes of this book, "bicycle" means mountain bike, usually with twenty-one speeds. Mountain bikes offer the extra durability and comfort required for Island touring. The prices shown are in Canadian dollars, with the higher range usually signifying greater durability.

Basics

If you already own a bike, you probably know more about them than I. I'm not a technician. Bikes are to ride, and perhaps maintain a little. However I'm fortunate in having an arrangement with Andrew Tuck, the owner of Bastion Cycle and Ski in Nanaimo, that seems to work for both of us. He tells me what I need, equips me with it, and repairs or replaces it when necessary. I write him cheques.

From Andrew I have learned that the basics of choosing a bike for cycle camping include considerations of price and size.

Price

You'll go just as far on a cheap bike, and nearly as fast — but you'll break down a lot more. Which is fine if you have lots of time and it happens in front of a pub. But not great if it's dark and raining, and you are two miles away from the last ferry sailing of the day.

A bike is the sum of its components. Generally, the higher the cost of the component, the more durable and reliable it will be. I have found that parts most difficult or impossible to repair on the road relate to shifters, derailleurs, brakes and bearings. These should be of average to good quality on a cycle being used to haul camping gear on the Island. Expect to pay between $600 and $800 for a cycle equipped with reasonable quality components. However even within this range, some bikes will have good frames and poor components, others the reverse. Try to find one with a combination of acceptable frame and components. Any reputable dealer can advise you on these.

Size

Size refers to frame size, and it is probably the most important specification to the average rider, since it is the basis of both comfort and efficiency. Frame sizes for adults will typically range between 16 and 22", a measure of roughly the distance between the axis on which the pedals rotate and the top of the seat tube. This range will accommodate most adults between 5'2" and 6'4". For example, I'm 6'4" and I ride a 20" frame. Again, a reputable dealer will be able to fit you with the best size.

The real keeners maintain there is a strong correlation between cycling efficiency and equipment weight. The frame and component manufacturers have accommodated that hypothesis by producing some very expensive, light-weight products. If you're racing a stripped down unit across back country to be first at the finish line, a five-kilogram weight advantage probably makes a huge difference. However Andrew informs me that at a certain point on the high-price/low-weight continuum, durability heads south as high price/low weight keeps going north.

Besides, most of my cycling buds will easily consume five kilos of beer and nachos in a day, negating all light-weight component advantages.

Modifications for Touring

There are some simple, low-tech changes which can be made to a stock bike to assist cycle camping. "Assist" means more comfort, and reduced fatigue. Both are critical where long travel days are planned, particularly when they are consecutive.

Three of these modifications relate to where body makes contact with bike — hands, seat and feet — and a fourth where the bike makes contact with the road.

Handlebar

The stock handlebar on a cycle is usually a more or less straight tube, with rubber grips at either end. This may be the optimum configuration for steering, I wouldn't know. However I do know from experience that this forces a terribly uncomfortable seating posture for prolonged touring. The rider has only one position for the hands, which restricts the arms and upper body to a single position. Over the course of the day this can be extremely fatiguing and sometimes painful, particularly to the wrists.

There are several corrective options. The simplest and least expensive is a pair of bar ends. These resemble cow horns that extend forward from the ends of the handle bar, offering an alternate gripping posture to relieve strain on the hands and wrists. They also stretch the body for more pedaling power, and the chance to rest a little by changing positions. Bar ends retail for $15–200; reasonable quality for $30–$50. They can easily be installed by the owner.

A more radical solution is to a replace the stock bar with any of the aftermarket versions that are made in shapes that can be grasped in a variety of locations. They retail for $40–$100, a price which can be partially offset by the sale of the stock bar. Since the upgrade is a little more complicated than adding bar ends, I suggest having it performed by the dealer, who will also provide a credit for the stock bar, if it is still new.

Regardless of your choice, be sure to have it wrapped in foam rubber grips. These enhance both comfort and grip, and isolate the rider from some of the banging and jarring associated with an irregular road surface ($8–$20 a set); I use two sets.

Seat

Over the course of a day's pedalling, particularly on consecutive days, a comfortable seat reduces fatigue, and generally contributes to positive frame of mind. I recommend upgrading to a gel seat, which distributes weight more evenly and more softly across the seat. I don't know why all bikes don't come with gel seats. If included at the time of purchase they are only about $40 over the price of the stock seat. Even purchased as a replacement item for an existing seat they are only $60.

I have learned that for me seat width is also a factor. My knees suffer from stretched cruciate ligaments, the result of too much physical activity on feet that are constructed in a manner which causes my legs to pronate. This is not a life-threatening condition, but under certain types of strain can be extremely painful.

Last summer, while training for an extended trip in the BC Interior, I replaced my worn-out gel seat with one that was a bit wider than my usual size. It was the last seat Andrew had in stock at the time. Shortly after this, on long rides my knees began to bother me. Several weeks later, on an impulse I traded with Alison for her slightly narrower seat. This seems to have reduced the pronating, because the knee pains disappeared and to date have not recurred.

Pedals

The keener's choice are clipless pedals, which greatly enhance pedaling efficiency by attaching the feet to the pedal cranks by specially designed interlocking fittings and shoes. We prefer pedals that accommodate shoes in which one can walk around when not cycling, eliminating the need to haul an extra pair. Consequently, we use decent quality pedals fitted with toe clips. The latter permit the feet to pull during the upward part of foot rotation (a help on hills, when I remember), and more importantly in my view, position them correctly for optimal pedalling efficiency. As an added benefit your feet can't slip off the pedals, preventing the introduction of groin to top tube.

Most stock pedals have a couple of screw holes to which the rider's choice of toe clips can be attached. Toe clips and straps retail for about $15.

When using pedals with toe clips, try to remember to remove at least one foot when coming to a stop.

Tires

The stock tires on all mountain bikes and many hybrids are "fat," knobby-tread, off-road tires. While these function reasonably well on pavement, they are designed mainly for traction in a variety of unpaved media.

We seldom ride off-road, so last year we replaced our stock tires with road tires. These feature narrower, thinner, straight-line treads which reduce roll resistance (pedal effort) with no compromise in ride comfort. According to my odometer we travel about 1.5 km per hour faster with these tires, a significant advantage on a 100-km day's travel.

Road tires cost from $15–$60, the latter amount for those reinforced with Kevlar, a substance which greatly resists punctures. I recently travelled 5000 km on Kevlar tires before incurring my first flat.

Accessories for Cycle Camping

Accessories transform the bike we have just created from a comfortable tourer to a comfortable tourer that can also haul gear. Enough gear, excluding the requirements of eating and laundry, to permit indefinite Island travel. Most of the accessories which follow I own and use. They are listed in descending (most to least) order of importance. The reader can feel free to disagree with my priorities.

Lock

I haven't heard of many bikes being stolen from pubs or campsites on the Island, but it does happen. Having spent $800 on a basic bike, upgraded it with $250 or so of options, and loaded it with several hundred dollars of camping gear, it's smart to keep it locked when not in use. The replacement value of my bike, fully loaded with personal possessions and camping gear is about $4,000.

Although locking won't prevent theft entirely, it will certainly discourage it. There are several good locks available. We favour the Kryptonite brand U-locks, that are key operated (a local high schooler who swore he wasn't a thief, once showed me how he could open a combination lock in less than two minutes), and of sufficient size that two bikes can be locked together. They retail for about $50. Avoid the much cheaper look-alikes; they are easily dismantled with bolt cutters or hack saws, the favourite tools of thieves.

Rear rack

Whether cycle camping or not, this is a most important accessory, because it is where the rider carries "stuff," usually with the aid of a bungee cord. The rack is used to hang panniers from, stack tents and bedding on, and generally haul anything too cumbersome to be contained in a pocket or hand. Don't leave home without one. Prices range from $8–$60, with reasonable quality for $35–$50.

Bungee cord

See "Rear rack" for use. I get by on a single cord that I've had for years. It is the right length to secure my tent, sleeping bag and mattress to my rack, with just enough slack to stuff in any last minute purchases, like a couple of steaks and a bottle of Beaujolais for the evening meal. Bungees break, so carrying a spare is a good idea. Prices range from $2 for a cord like mine to $10 for a more elaborate "split cord," which secures the load with two strands instead of one.

Water bottles and cages

I carry two bottles in cages screwed to my frame in pre-drilled holes. Because I perspire so much I use the largest I can buy. In one I keep plain water, to drink and also wash sweat from my head and face. In the other I store a mixture of water and juice for rehydration and an energy boost. $12–$20 per set.

Rear panniers

"Pannier" is French for "basket." Depending of your choice of "basket," it can be English for anything from "bliss" to "downright irritating." Most personal possessions are carried in the rear panniers, whose capacity are a function of overall volume and number of individual compartments. Considerations when selecting a pannier include:

- *quality of construction* — strength of fabric, and durability of hardware.
- *method of attachment* — each should be secure at three points, two on the rack, and a third lower, usually a hook on the rack support slightly above the rear axle. They should remain attached on bumpy surfaces and not obstruct the rider's heels.
- *design* — "side" opening permits easier access to the interior while mounted on a fully loaded bike than "top" opening. Extra outside compartments facilitate storing and locating frequently used items.
- *intended use* — I use my panniers a lot, tend to overstuff them, and because I lack patience, can be a little rough opening and closing compartment zippers. My last set of panniers failed at the zippers and mounting brackets one year after purchase. My wife's identical set is still fine.

The reader will note that I have not included waterproof as a criterion. For many cyclists this is not an issue, either because they don't cycle in the rain, they wrap their gear in waterproof bags, or their panniers, due to their quality of construction, possess a high degree of water resistance.

However I hasten to add that because I cycle camp year-round, my new panniers are waterproof. Nothing which they contain can possibly get wet. However they have only one compartment, meaning no quick access to identification, beer money, etc., and they are expensive. Alternatively, on hot summer days each is easily emptied and filled with ice to convert to a temporary campsite refrigerator.

Panniers can be purchased for as low as $30 a set, and as high as $300. Avoid the former. Expect to pay $100–$150 for some that will last.

Seat pouch

This handy little device attaches to the underside of the seat and seat post. Mine contains much of my tool kit, where it is out of the way, but accessible when needed. $30 will buy an adequate version.

Handlebar pouch

We each added one to our accessories this year. Mine is a small, but expandable and at various time holds wallet, spare cash, maps, gloves and any interesting bits and pieces that I find along the roadside. Alison's is larger and more expensive, and was purchased for the Ireland trip to contain purse, camera, passport, etc. Depending on size and number of pockets, $40–$60 or more.

Odometer

I've had one of these little gizmos for years. While it has several functions, those which I use most are distance travelled and average speed. This is helpful information on long trips, because it facilitates calculating remaining distance and ETA.

It also informs me of my current and maximum speeds, and time — mostly curiosity items.

Mine cost about $40. More elaborate units which also measure heart rate, cadence, etc., can be as high as $200.

Front panniers

I'm sure that many riders would not place front panniers so low on their priority lists. However we've only recently purchased ours so have little experience with them, and we seem to have fared well for years without them.

We bought them for two reasons. The first was to increase carrying capacity on extended trips (front panniers are slightly smaller versions of rear panniers). The second was to permit the forward transfer of heavy camping items (stove, cookware, etc.). This relieves the weight over the back wheel, which to this point has been burdened by both rider and gear.

The early reviews are mixed. They proved difficult to install properly, but greatly increase carrying capacity and compromise steering very little. A pleasant surprise has been the increased stability when pedaling standing up, the result of more effective weight distribution. Prices for acceptable quality range from $75–$150.

Handlebar mounted entertainment centre

Last summer we actually encountered a fellow with a radio, cassette player and right and left speakers built onto his handlebar. That evening our fascination with this set-up was somewhat abetted by his commitment to sharing his boorish music with a crowded campground. Upon my request he turned it off. Sometimes people listen to guys that ride 20' frames.

I apologize for having no picture of this remarkable accessory.

Tool Kit

There are two components to any tool kit: the tools themselves and the ability to use them. For years at Andrew's recommendation, I carried a chain tool, which theoretically allowed me to remove and replace broken links. Also, in the event of a broken rear derailleur it enables one to shorten the chain to create a one speed, and make it home. I was blessed with never needing to use this device, which was fortunate. When I finally decided to

The two Davids repairing a tire — anytime!

use it to remove my chain for cleaning, fortunately at home, I found I didn't know how. Several hours and wrecked links later I figured it out. Had this been needed for an emergency repair on a cold, wet road in the middle of nowhere, I would not have been a happy camper.

During the past three years my bike and I have travelled eighteen thousand kilometres, most on the Island, and many loaded with camping gear. Below, in descending order of frequency, are things that have gone wrong:

Flat tires — punctured or pinched inner tubes. Punctures can happen at any time. On the Island roads they are usually caused by metal and glass fragments. Pinched inner tubes are caused by insufficient tire pressure and are easily repaired.

Destroyed tires — the result of contact with large sharp objects; often avoidable.

Loose spokes — resulting in warped and dangerously unstable wheels.

Broken spoke(s) — see loose spokes.

Loosened seat — front rides up and gets a little uncomfortable for my reproductive equipment.

Loosened accessories — excluding the aforementioned reproductive equipment, these included rear rack, bottle cages, pannier attachments, lights and reflectors.

Broken/bent chain links — caused by making a really sloppy front gear change while ascending a steep hill.

Bent rim — caused by a large dog which inexplicably passed quickly between my front wheel and frame. The front wheel was pretzeled beyond repair. We abandoned the trip. The dog was fine.

Worn-out brake pads — can occur rapidly on extended hilly trips during which much rain is encountered.

My tool kit combines awareness of the above contingencies with my lack of mechanical skill. It includes:

- patch kit ($5)
- spare inner tube ($4–$30)
- spare tire (extended trips only, $15–$60)
- three tire levers ($6)
- small hand pump ($40, don't buy a cheap one)
- spoke adjuster ($8)
- chain tool ($20, don't buy a cheap one)
- set of Allen keys ($17)
- small adjustable wrench ($10)
- spare brake pads (extended trips only, $6–$30)
- chain lubricant ($12)
- Swiss army knife ($35)

Most of this fits in my seat pouch. We own several cycling guides that recommend tool kits that are far more extensive. However when cycle camping, carrying capacity is limited, and I prefer to leave some room for essentials like my hand-held TV.

Cycling Clothing

It is easy for those of us with middle-aged minds and bodies to think of specialized cycling apparel only as those loud close-fitting styles worn by posturing younger folks to flaunt their flat tummies and tiny behinds. In fact today's rider can choose from a range of specialty clothing, close or loose fitting, gaudily coloured or sedate. Regardless of style it offers comfort and durability.

Pants

I carry at least one pair each of short and long pants. Each has padding where my seat contacts the bike's. Even with a gel seat (the bike's, not mine) I still recommend padded cycling pants.

Incidentally, I own a pair of close fitting lycra pants, and even if they aren't figure flattering, they are by far the most comfortable pants I own for cycling. Besides, I don't have to look at myself in them.

Shirt

In warm weather I wear a simple cotton T. It gets pretty sweaty at the end of each day, but can be rinsed out and tied to my pack to dry. For cool days I have a couple of polypropylene, long-sleeved shirts which keep me warm while "wicking" sweat away from my skin.

Jacket

There are several brands of micro fiber jackets available which are warm, light, wind and water repellent, and compress well for easy storage. Some have a fold-down rear flap for protection from mud thrown by the rear wheel.

As a safety precaution they come in bright, neon colours to enhance visibility.

Shoes

Cycling shoes are a must for the long distance tourer. In addition to being light-weight, their soles are more rigid than walking shoes. This reduces flexing in the feet when pedaling, ensuring a more efficient energy transfer from rider to bike. To the rider this means less fatigue at the end of the day.

If you wish to avoid carrying an extra pair for walking around, buy a pair of cycling shoes with a slightly more flexible sole and wider tread.

Helmet

I began wearing a helmet about five years ago. Even after trying a couple of different styles and weights, I still dislike them. However I wear mine most of the time. Too much can go wrong when on a bike. Beginning in 1996, cyclists in BC are required by law to wear helmets.

Gloves

I've tried specially padded cycling gloves, and they make some difference in comfort, but not a lot. This is probably because my handle bars are so well padded.

However I do carry a pair of old woolen gloves for cold or wet days. Wool is a particularly good insulator when wet. We've pedaled in some pretty miserable (for us) winter weather, and my hands have yet to get cold. Bike stores sell synthetically insulated gloves which perform as well for considerably more money.

Socks

Haven't found a pair yet that keep my feet either warm or dry in cold or wet weather, regardless of the manufacturers' claims. I use cotton socks on warm days and woollies on cold ones.

Booties

In anticipation of Ireland's rain we each recently bought a pair of these, which cover the shoes to keep feet dry. For the most part they accomplish this; they also keep feet warm when it is not raining. We should have owned some years ago.

Tips

Alison has a degree in physical and health education, and she's an athlete. Mine is in political science, and I'm not. However these skills are not as disparate as they may seem. When she explains to me how it is that I've just damaged my body yet again, I can usually understand. And frequently remember.

Never, never, never permit your fatigue to reach exhaustion

When cycling distances, particularly loaded down, it is common to be tired. Fatigue is a product of physical effort, often accompanied by dehydration. Rest often, and take fluids continuously. Our group is pretty fit, and depending on conditions we rest every ten to fifteen kilometres, sometimes more frequently. Be assured that if you push yourself to exhaustion, regardless of the amount of rest you get that evening and whether you are unfit, a little fit, or mostly fit you will pay the next day, and sometimes longer.

Watch what you drink

Not all fluids rehydrate. Plain water, juice or a mixture are the best. Carbonated drinks, tea, coffee and alcohol can cause water loss, depriving the body of fluids when it most needs them.

Maintain a steady cadence and let your gears do the work

Find a rate of foot rotation that you can sustain comfortably. As terrain changes to increase or lower pedal resistance, select a gear that will accommodate your cadence. Standing up will provide more leverage and permits the use of different muscles, while resting those previously in use. However this technique raises the centre of gravity and adversely affects the stability of a loaded bike and rider.

Inflate tires to the manufacturer's suggested maximum

The slight, if any, reduction in comfort will be more than offset by the increased efficiency from reduced roll resistance. Also, hard tires will sustain greater loads and are far less susceptible to flats than soft ones.

Our roads can be slippery when wet

While we sometimes complain about the amount of rain the Island receives, we often experience weeks on end when none falls. All the automotive oils and fluids deposited by our considerable traffic flow are absorbed by the asphalt. When the rains finally return, these deposits become a dangerous surface slick, particularly at intersections.

Spoke wear is insidious

Most spoke wear is impossible to see. It occurs in the curve of the spoke that is attached to the hub, particularly in the rear wheel which is both a drive and load-bearing wheel. The spoke literally saws through, with the first symptom usually being that a single spoke will break. This invariably leads to rim distortion which if unattended will render the bike inoperable, sometimes within a short distance. It also means that the remaining spokes are ready to go.

Get to a bicycle store and change them all. It won't be inexpensive but is guaranteed to avoid much grief. I know this from personal experience.

Weather and wind

The Island and many of its main roads lie in a north-west to south-east direction. Depending on direction of travel, the weather can be a help or hindrance. Specifically, rain is usually accompanied by south-east winds, which can be quite brisk in the late fall, winter and early spring. Heading up-Island (north) they can be such a boon that one is prepared to ignore the precipitation. Alternatively, cycling down-Island means bucking a head wind in driving rain.

Clear weather arrives from the north, facilitating down-Island travel. Several times each summer we experience very strong north winds. These are a result of extended hot and sunny weather in the province's interior, which causes its surface air to rise rapidly, sucking coastal air down the Strait of Georgia like a giant vacuum cleaner.

Cycling south in these conditions is like a sleigh ride; north like travelling uphill all day. Sometimes departing early (i.e., at sunrise), helps.

Riding at night

BC law requires the use of a headlight and rear light from one hour after sunset to one hour before sunrise. Offenders are fined.

EQUIPMENT: CAMPING GEAR

From the moment I thought of creating this book, this was the chapter to which I most looked forward to writing, because I actually have some knowledge of the subject.

Colleen Roy, who with her husband Larry operates North Island Water Sports in Nanaimo, and I have a relationship similar to my arrangement with Andrew at the bike store. Colleen is an awesome salesperson. She convinces me I need an item, sometimes by lending to one of my friends something she thinks I should buy. This renders me incapable of getting along without it. Then I give her money.

I have learned over the years that choice of camping equipment is governed by only two considerations: intended use and frequency of use. Because I cycle camp year-round on the Island, the design and construction of my equipment differs from that of, for example the weekend car camper. As with bicycles, camping equipment is best purchased from a reputable dealer who can assist with selection. Colleen and Larry are also continuously testing new gear. So they serve their customers as an ongoing reference resource for tips and equipment.

The inexperienced camper will undoubtedly be puzzled by the range and prices of similar appearing equipment offered by various retailers. Buyer beware. Items which look alike, but with huge differences in price probably have equally huge differences in the quality of design, materials and construction. Resist the urge to purchase cheap equipment. It will fail you.

The descriptions which follow reflect choices that have evolved from my research and experience.

Shelter

Tent

In preparing the text for this section I just realized that we have owned eight tents since getting married. Not one of them has been lost or destroyed. Each was replaced as evolving designs and materials made the newer designs irresistible.

For example, our latest tent pitches in minutes, doesn't need pegs, has a fly which doubles as a storage vestibule, sleeps two comfortably, and is always warm and dry. It packs to 14 x 46 cm and weighs only 2.13 kg. It cost about $300. Some of the features that we have learned to appreciate when cycle camping include:

- light weight and small packed volume, which reduce fatigue and save space.
- free-standing design, eliminating the need for some or all tent pegs. Parts of the Island have very shallow surface soil, meaning poor or no holding for pegs.
- an outside frame to which the tent is attached by clips rather than sleeves. This translates to a tent with superior ventilation, less potential for interior condensation and acceptable interior height. It can also be assembled very quickly — important if you are cold, tired and cranky.

Sleeping bag

A sleeping bag for cycle camping on the Island should:

- provide warmth through the range of temperatures experienced on the Island, which in fact is pretty narrow. It seldom exceeds 25°C in the summer, or drops below -5°C in winter. It is always cool at night, particularly near the ocean.
- continue to provide insulation when damp, or even soaking wet. This requirement eliminates bags filled with natural substances such as cotton or down, which lose most of their insulation when wet.
- stuff to a manageable size to facilitate transport on a bike rack.

A bag of reasonable quality that will provide comfort in any Island season will contain synthetic insulation (for example Thinsulate, Lite Loft or Hollofil) which retains most of its insulation when wet, and weighs about 2 kg. When packed for travel, particularly in a stuff sack, these sleeping bags compress to a surprisingly small volume. Prices will vary from $180 to $300.

Many manufacturers offer a choice of left- or right-side zippers. If you plan to travel regularly with the same conjugal other, consider buying one of each. Then you can zip them together to facilitate cuddling.

Mattress

To my mind there is only one acceptable mattress, the Thermarest, which is self-inflating and made in several lengths, thicknesses, and foam densities. They are all warm, comfortable, light and durable, and roll up to a manageable size for hauling. Thermarests are composed of an airtight shell filled with compressed foam that expands when air is introduced by opening a small valve at one end. They retail for about $100.

There are other types of mattress on the market, most less expensive. Don't consider them. We've owned our thermarests for ten years and have used them from northern Ontario in the winter to the Mojave desert, with only one small puncture that was easily repaired.

We also own a "couple kit" that permits the mattresses to be joined together on nights when Alison and I are speaking to each other.

Cooking and Eating Utensils

Cooking and eating tools are not essential to cycle camping on the Island. There are usually eateries en route. Terry, who is no gourmet diner, enjoys the cycling, camping and pubbing but prefers to buy packaged fast food during the day rather than cook his own. Usually he remembers to remove the cellophane wrapping before he eats it. However most in our group are sufficiently traditional and sociable that we enjoy the opportunity to prepare and share meals together at the beginning and end of each day.

An itemization of the articles in my kit, which has evolved over the years, follows. Its components are compact, durable and light, simple, and easy to clean. For reasons of space and weight they are only included if they are going to be used. Because I'm always on the lookout for new gear, and anxious to remain ahead of David Moddle (cycling companion and squash opponent) in the "gadget wars," new suggestions are welcomed.

Stacking cook set

This assembly contains two pots and lids, a fry pan, and the wind screen for my stove, all contained in the largest pot, as is the burner of my two piece stove. My set is stainless steel, which is heavier than aluminum, but more resistant to dents, easier to clean and less conducive to memory loss.

It retails for about $60 and easily meets the food preparation needs of two campers.

Cookware is also now available with non-stick surfaces. As yet I don't own any, but suspect this is a good idea. Many of my more ambitious attempts at campsite cuisine have had to be chipped from the bottom of the pan. Presumably this can be avoided with non-stick cookware.

Stoves

Stoves can be purchased as one- (burner and tank combined) and two-piece (burner connected to the fuel reservoir by a hose) units. Fuels include white gas (naphtha), kerosene, propane, alcohol, and latterly unleaded gasoline. While some stoves burn more than one fuel, this is not an essential feature on the Island because all the aforementioned types are readily attainable.

When choosing a stove, factors to consider include volume and weight, availability of parts, availability of fuel, ease of lighting (particularly when cold), ease of repair in the field, and fuel efficiency. There are various domestic and imported makes priced from $50–$100. Because in my experience all are suitable for Island camping, choice will be mostly a function of personal priorities.

Over the years we have owned only two stoves — first a one-piece white gas burner, and recently a two-piece version of the same stove. We purchased the two piece partly because our research revealed that it was lighter, and carried a higher volume of fuel. And partly because my Mom had given me $80 for Xmas and I was keen to own this gadget ahead of Moddle.

After three seasons it has performed as well as the one piece, and burns longer between refills. But it occupies more pack volume, is fragile, has more moving parts, and is difficult to repair in the field.

Partly as a result of researching this book I have decided to return to exclusive use of the one piece. Although it needs more frequent refills, it's smaller and tougher.

Eating utensils

When travelling alone, my eating utensils frequently comprise only a cup, knife, fork and spoon. The articles in my cook set double as plates and bowls. In addition to minimizing pack weight and volume, this arrangement also lessens dishwashing, a chore which I detest.

When travelling accompanied, to permit my cook set to be shared, I carry utensils which include:

plate — stainless steel, durable and easy to clean ($10)

cup — stainless steel, double wall, vacuum insulated ($23)

bowl/sierra cup — stainless steel ($6)

knife, fork and spoon — lexan, light, tough and cheap ($5)

Other Accessories

This is the field in which the serious gadget wars are fought. I have tried to arrange them in order of priority, but modified by the need to stay competitive. In fact some I may not even own, but couldn't resist the urge to include, just to get into Moddle's head. The mature reader's list may differ significantly from mine.

sheath knife — sees continuous use for bike repairs, campfires, food preparation, etc. My preference is a rigid, stainless steel blade that holds its edge well, and a non-slip, even when wet, handle ($50).

cork screw — if you need an explanation, this book will serve you no further use ($5).

candle lantern — compact, reliable, and romantic (a lot like myself). These emit just enough light by which to read, and to prevent tripping over nearby obstacles. Although the practice is considered unsafe, I frequently suspend mine inside my tent for reading comfort when the weather outside is poor ($25). Candles, which burn for 6 – 8 hours, are about $.75 each.

small flashlight — for short-term and emergency uses ($20).

small hatchet — compact, light and essential for splitting firewood, particularly in provincial parks where wood is free but hard and comes in big pieces ($17).

Sven saw — an efficient, light and compact folding tool for bucking fallen branches. Unfortunately the teeth protrude slightly when folded ($25). (I suspect this was what punctured my Thermarest.)

dishwashing kit — zip-lock bag with small container of biodegradable soap and scouring pad. Add two willing hands and the largest pot in your kit, and you have a dishwasher.

fuel bottle — light-weight aluminum canister(s), 1 – 2 litre capacities ($15 – $20). A built-in pour spout will save fuel lost to spillage ($5).

spatula — Alison insisted I include this.

Outback Oven — converts stove to oven. We have baked pizza, potatos, bread and quiche in ours. Also saves fuel by heating pots faster ($50).

stainless steel thermos — holds about three cups. Great for carrying a warm drink on cold days. And for making coffee at night, to drink in bed in the morning ($50).

hand-held TV — ideal at night when travelling alone ($175).

small lantern — white gas, for seasons when daylight is short ($50). Take lots of spare mantles, cycling is hard on them ($1.50 each).

watch that includes barometer and altimeter — assists with predicting inclement weather, and also provides ammunition for bragging about hills ($90).

compact binoculars — great for closer views of the mountains, ocean, wildlife, and the antics of other campers, without appearing nosy ($120).

book light — battery-operated book attachment for reading in bed. New this year. My owning this should bring Moddle to his knees. Free, for a limited time, when purchasing photocopier toner.

miniature espresso maker — I bought this mainly to drive you-know-who nuts. Turns out he was the only one of us that likes espresso, so I gave it to him ($35).

plastic lighter — while I carry matches, I use this little device when my matches are damp or difficult to light due to weather. And they are free, having been dropped at roadsides by smoking hitch-hikers who haven't yet figured out that in Canada bus fare is a lot cheaper than cigarettes.

water filter — this removes suspensions, bacteria and viruses through a combination of charcoal and ceramic filters, and sometimes iodine. I bought mine, a small pocket version, this year after cycling north of Sayward. It was very hilly and hot, mostly uninhabited, and there was no water available at rest stops. I was reduced to begging water from travellers.

The alternative was to drink from the numerous roadside streams, from which giardia (beaver fever) is a constant possibility. A water filter would have eliminated this threat, which reduces a cycling trip to a series of short jaunts connected by visits to the washroom ($70).

miscellaneous — watertight case for matches, plastic bags to keep articles dry, small plastic containers for margarine and peanut butter, insect repellent (we have few bugs; I seldom use mine), tent and Thermarest repair kits.

Cooking (yes or no?)

This book nearly went to the publisher without a section on cooking. Then one morning as I sat in a cafe while conducting field research north of Campbell River, it occurred to me that eating, for which cooking can be a prerequisite, is pretty important and needed to be addressed. Below are my hastily scribbled thoughts of that morning, while awaiting my omelette. They describe my usual eating routine while on the road, which reflects my idiosyncrasies and budget.

The culinary options usually available to the cycling camper on the Island are to eat at restaurants (mostly roadside cafes) or pubs, buy groceries en route, or carry packaged meals.

Cafes and pubs

With the exception of the extreme northern end, these abound at regular intervals in most areas of the Island. I frequently have breakfast in cafes, particularly when travelling alone. I do this primarily for two reasons. First, I like to ease my way into the day, minimizing my morning chores. Packing up mattress, sleeping bag and tent is enough. The preparation of breakfast-for- one at a campsite is an excessive drain on my morning energy.

Secondly, a cafe breakfast at the start of the day's ride permits the use of a flush facility, thereby avoiding the dreaded pit toilet. The reader planning to emulate this sequence will appreciate that correct timing is critical, and may require several attempts to perfect.

For reasons that are apparent in this book, I always have lunch at a pub. In fact I plan my route and agenda to include this.

Buying groceries

Groceries purchased en route provide cost advantages over cafe, pub and packaged food. They also offer the flexibility of being able to prepare the specific foods that will meet the wants of the moment, particularly if these are fresh vegetables, fruits or meats. The disadvantages relate mainly to their sometimes cumbersome volume and weight, and the possibility of spoilage.

We often prepare supper from groceries bought at the last store before reaching our campsite.

Packaged meals

These are the freeze-dried and dehydrated variety. They have improved immensely since first appearing on the market, at which time they tasted mostly like salt with a hint of food flavouring.

A quick reference to one of my commercial equipment catalogues revealed a selection of over seventy-five dinner entrees, breakfasts, desserts, side dishes and snacks, many of which are vegetarian. Most are packaged as two-portion servings, occupy little space and weight, and frequently require little more than some water and a little time to prepare. We have found the servings to be tasty and quite generous, while meeting the high energy nutrition requirements of cycling. Three meals a day for two people cost $20–25, slightly more expensive than groceries, but far less than restaurants.

If desired, a cyclist could easily pack a week's meals of these foods. Some are available as single portions, and have become my preferred method of preparing supper when travelling alone.

Included under the heading of packaged foods are also the pre-packaged ingredients for baking in the Outback Oven, a lightweight kit which converts a single-burner camp stove to an oven. In the year since we bought ours we have baked bread, cake, pizza, potatoes, and quiche, mostly successfully.

We have also learned that preparing food in this device offers opportunities for a few laughs. The extended preparation time affords the chance to socialize — perhaps with some wine, although this can be a detriment. One evening, with the help of a delightful Riesling, my friend Judy made focaccia bread. Having unwittingly kneaded an unopened capsule of olive oil into the dough, she also neglected to allow any time for rising. We baked it anyway. Later it had to be chipped from the bottom of the pan.

Clothing

For weeks I procrastinated writing this section, without really stopping to analyze why. To this point there had always been more interesting and easier topics on which to write. Having now exhausted these I am compelled to address the subject of clothing, which is probably of interest to many readers.

I shall begin by attempting to analyze why this subject so intimidates me. For starters, while I recognize the importance of carrying appropriate clothing, I find describing it truly boring. To any of you who remember in high school having to write a 250-word essay on the imagery in an Emily Dickenson poem, that's how I feel now.

Secondly, the modern outdoorsperson expects his/her clothing to fulfill several needs — provide comfort and protection from the elements, and make a fashion statement. The weighting placed on these needs by the wearer is intensely personal, and varies greatly between consumers. Consequently the range of clothing offered by manufacturers is immense, and to me, daunting. A trip to any sporting goods store supports this view. A large portion, if not the majority, of floor space is dedicated to fashion.

Finally, people react to physical exertion, of which cycling is a form, and the elements differently. For example, my body heats up quickly and I perspire profusely. Unlike some of my pals I do not enjoy hot weather, but am largely unaffected by the cool weather in which some are quite uncomfortable. These sorts of personal differences make generalized recommendations for specific types of clothing difficult.

I am reluctant to term the description which follows "recommendations." Rather it refers to clothing, in addition to the cycling duds mentioned in an earlier chapter, which I and my companions have found to be effective. Factors that influenced selection, other than fashion and personal physiology, include the range of weather likely to be encountered, weight and packed volume.

assorted T-shirts, socks and underwear — these occupy little volume or weight, even if carried in large numbers, and are easily washed and dried en route.

fleece jacket or vest, and pants — light weight, easily compressed for packing, warm (even when wet) and quick drying. Island evenings, even during the summer can be cool and damp. Alison carries and uses her fleece clothing year round.

hooded sweat shirt — even though this occupies a lot of packed volume, it is my favourite campsite apparel. The hood restricts lost body heat, the front pouch is a convenient hand warmer, and it rolls up nicely as a pillow for sleeping.

wind pants — these light shells greatly assist with keeping legs warm.

Gore-tex jacket — waterproof, light, warm and extremely comfortable. The fabric "breathes," keeping the wearer dry in any weather.

other — walking shorts, sweat pants, woolen gloves, toque.

Helpful hints:

- always keep handy a dry, warm, complete change of clothing in which to change upon reaching camp at the end of the day. We have found this to be refreshing and energizing, regardless of the weather encountered during the trip.
- avoid wearing cotton garments in cold, damp weather. Damp cotton functions as a heat exchanger, transferring much needed body heat into the surrounding air.

The reader will be pleased to note that, should it be necessary to add any articles to a clothing inventory, these can probably be purchased at a reasonable price en route. In particular Victoria, Duncan, Nanaimo, Courtenay, and Campbell River all have abundant clothing and sportswear stores.

First Aid Kit

It had not occurred to me to write a section on first aid. Mishaps haven't been a significant part of my cycling or camping experiences. However, my daughter Kristin, who knows everything by virtue of being twenty and having completed three years of university, recently counselled that I should have a first aid kit.

I have previously included reference to my tool kit, which I suppose is first aid for bikes, so for the sake of consistency I will recount some of the incidents that I have experienced while cycling or camping, and which have influenced the contents of my first aid kit.

trips over the handlebars — usually off-road at low speed. The result of inexperience and/or poor judgment. The landings can cause the odd scratch, and some discomfort for a couple of days.

scorched eyebrows and lashes — from leaning too close while lighting a pressurized camp stove for which I had recently incorrectly replaced the generator. The resultant concern was mostly for the surrounding trees and homes.

hunting knife dropped into calf muscle — obviously caused by an error in design by the sheath manufacturer. Some pain. Stitches, had they been available, would have been nice. Boot lace tourniquet, aspirin and scotch didn't do the job I had expected. In fact there was an unexpected delay at the hospital the next day over the possibility of gangrene.

concussion — the fault of a large-diameter wet log that refused to be overriden; exacerbated by toe clips that would not release my feet. For those old enough to remember, the little man in the raincoat capsizing his tricycle on "Laugh In" comes to mind. The ensuing month of short-term memory loss was a nuisance.

falling sideways from bike — usually occurs on-road, with no warning, as a result of wheels failing to adhere to the surface. Some of these can really, really hurt.

My bottom line on accidents is that they are going to be either serious or not. If not, they will be helped by some cleaning, dressing, and perhaps a little pain killer. If serious, there is very little which can be done short of flagging down a vehicle for a trip to the nearest hospital.

My first aid kit reflects the above contingencies combined with my lack of maturity. It includes:

Band-Aids (various sizes)
Rubbing alcohol (or hydrogen peroxide)
Aspirin
BC Health Care Card

EQUIPMENT: PUBS

The reader may be skeptical of the notion of pubs as equipment — but think about it. A main objective in choosing a bike is comfort. THE goal of camping is comfort. And what does one seek in a pub? You've got it — comfort.

Nobody in his right mind would settle-in anywhere to indulge in a couple of cold ones and scoff a plate of fries if he weren't comfortable. Fortunately, during the course of my research for this book I found not a single pub that lacked comfort.

Pubs on the Island exist primarily in either of two forms — as components of hotels, or as stand-alone neighbourhood pubs. The hotels are frequently older buildings, sometimes dating back to the 1800s when they served as inns to stagecoach and early rail travellers. As such they were integral to that era's transportation infrastructure. Others were grand establishments built to serve their communities during their highly prosperous resource-based infancies. The interior walls of many are adorned with photographs of those early days, historical reminders of different times. Few actually now offer overnight accommodation. Their rooms remain vacant, and exist only to facilitate retention of their liquor licenses.

Many hotel owners and managers take pride in preserving the historic atmosphere of their buildings, and have also researched their pasts. When not too occupied with serving customers they will usually be pleased to regale the visitor with details of the local community's history, of which the pub was often a central component.

A minority of hotel pubs are best described as beer parlours, and while they serve their clientele well, offer all the ambience of a railway station washroom. Beer parlours don't really bother me, and when travelling alone I sometimes frequent them because they offer great people-watching. However I have omitted reference to them in my book because their sights, sounds and smells will lack appeal to many. Perhaps in a future edition I'll include a section on those pubs in which the typical cyclist will never wish to set foot.

Neighbourhood pubs are so designated because they are intended to serve the adult population within a specific radius. In fact, before a pub can be built-majority approval of the adults living within that radius must be obtained. Now a British Columbia fixture, they have only been around for about twenty years. Before then, hosting legal social drinking outside the home was supposed to have been only an ancillary activity of establishments with a nobler primary role, such as hotels, clubs and restaurants. At some point the politicians came to believe that we could be trusted with institutions intended mainly as venues in which to imbibe. Following a tentative start, during which we confirmed our trustworthiness, neighbourhood pubs have proliferated throughout the province.

As recently as ten years ago ownership of a neighbourhood pub was sure to be pretty lucrative. However, the recent emphases on healthy eating, reduced alcohol consumption, lower disposable incomes, and cocooning have changed this. To their credit many owners have responded with expanded and reasonably priced menus, large servings, excellent service, evening entertainment, and companion wine- and beer-retail outlets. The latter offer the opportunity to purchase a six-pack or bottle of wine to share later around the camp fire.

The pubs described in this book have been chosen for two reasons, First, over time they have proved to be located at a place where it is convenient and timely to take a break, or stop for the day. Second, one feels comfortable patronizing them, by virtue of decor, service or menu.

Some pub facts that may be helpful to a newcomer to the province:

- they are usually, though not necessarily always, open from 11 A.M. to 11 P.M., seven days a week.
- all permit smoking; many have very effective air purifying systems.
- many have outdoor seating, usually May through September.
- their atmospheres, and dress codes are always casual; shoes and shirts, please.
- most serve a variety of ciders, ales, Pilsners and lagers, several on tap, often the product of a local micro-brewery.

Tips

English-style pubs

This designation means bar service only. It's a good idea to ask, or you could get mighty thirsty sitting at a table waiting to be served.

Water bottle refills

Bartenders will gladly fill your water bottle with water and chipped ice for the next leg of your trip.

Security

Pubs seldom provide bicycle security, presumably because there is currently no economic incentive to do so. However we have found pub staff to be extremely cooperative in providing a safe place for the owner concerned about theft.

The Horseshoe Bay Inn in Chemainus fronts directly onto a busy street, and if it's not too crowded inside, I take my bike in with me. I talk to my bike a lot, so it doesn't seem unusual when I order her a beer.

Cash advances

Recently I have noted that hotel pubs in particular allow their patrons cash advances on bank cards (Interac). This is especially convenient when no ATM is nearby.

Campgrounds

The Island abounds in campsites. Those described in this book are my favourites, primarily because their locations complement my cycle routes. They are mostly provincial parks and private resorts. However it is to be noted that there are dozens of alternate choices available to the camper. Details of these can be found in a variety of guides, all free at tourist information centres.

Several municipalities also maintain public campgrounds, as do the BC Forest Service and logging companies, these usually in more remote areas. The Island also has one national park, Pacific Rim National Park

Provincial Parks

These frequently occupy areas of natural or ecological significance, are usually heavily treed and include a network of hiking paths in addition to the designated camping areas. Although some can be quite large with one hundred or more sites, density is low, permitting reasonable privacy. Reservations at selected Island provincial parks can be made by phoning 1-800-689-9025. Otherwise sites are allocated on a first-come, first-served basis. In the summer the popular parks fill up very quickly, often by mid-afternoon, sometimes sooner.

Provincial campsites include at least the following facilities:

- designated level sites, including picnic table and fire pit
- a nearby crib containing firewood (empty when campfires are banned due to forest fire hazard, a frequent summer occurrence)
- a nearby cold water tap or pump
- my all-time favourite, the pit toilet

Some provincial parks, particularly the large ones, offer flush toilets and showers.

A pamphlet entitled "Provincial Parks of Vancouver Island" can be obtained free at any travel information centre. This details the location, size and amenities of each provincial park, which can also include nature interpretive centres and lectures, information brochures, and a park host to assist with any questions.

Expect to pay between $10 and $16 per night in a provincial park. Fee schedules are uniform throughout the province and are a function of the amenities provided.

Private campgrounds

Private campgrounds are often part of resorts, which will also rent guest cabins and spaces for recreation vehicles. They are destination points in themselves and frequently include use of a swimming pool and recreation area in the camping fee. These are not usually as esthetically pleasing as provincial parks, but often have a greater range of services, usually on a user-pay basis. They can include:

- coin-operated laundry
- pay phone
- ice
- groceries and camping supplies
- washrooms with hot water, coin-operated showers

Many campers prefer the more "wilderness like" surroundings of provincial parks. However, I have learned that after a particularly tough day on the road, extra amenities like a hot shower and cold pop are welcome. And the proximity to fellow campers often leads to the opportunity to make new acquaintances and exchange experiences.

Private site fees are in the area of those charged by the provincial parks or a little higher. I have paid as high as $25. While price gouging by private operators is rare, I have experienced it, mainly in the Tofino area. Demand there is high, facilities are limited and alternate accommodation a considerable distance away.

Forest Service and logging company campsites

By design these facilities are in remote areas, usually accessible only by logging road. They are typically small, around ten sites, with only a fire ring and pit toilet as conveniences, and are often located at the side of a lake or river.

Most are currently free of charge, although some have begun to collect a site fee to cover the costs of security and garbage collection.

Other

On one of our trips we met an amazing couple from London, England who had just completed cycling the entire length of South America. Having no jobs to which they could return in England, they decided to take the time to cycle across Canada, presumably on limited funds. They regularly camped in rest areas, a practice which I thought was illegal.

From their research they had determined that overnight camping was permitted in rest areas, provided no signs were posted to prohibit it. They waited until after 8:00 P.M. before setting up camp, and left early in the morning.

TIPS

Campground full

Some campgrounds maintain designated hiker/biker areas in which there is always room. So even if the sign at the entrance reads "campground full," it's still a good idea to ask if there is room for cyclists.

Management will often give a break to campers with small tents by allowing two for the price of one, provided they stay in the same site.

Critters

Particularly in provincial parks and forest service sites, keep food away from animals. These can range from cute but irritating (raccoons and ravens), to downright dangerous (bears and cougars), to strange (a mink once undid our food pack and tunneled through most of the length of a baguette).

Usually it is effective to contain food securely in a closed pack. However if bears are in the area it is advisable to suspend food at least three metres above ground from a tree branch. If a cougar is bothering campers, an almost unheard of event, it is assuredly infirm and desperate. Leave! A cougar attack will ruin your day. The proximity of dangerous animals to a campground will often, but not always be accompanied by warning signs, and cautions from park staff.

Under no circumstances should food, or anything that an animal might consider food, like toothpaste, ever be taken into a tent. The scent will linger for years.

Bugs

Insect bites are a small issue here in paradise. There is a minor black fly presence in some areas in late spring and early summer. In spots where there are mosquitoes, these confine their bite times to an hour or two in the evening. I have also experienced no-see-ums at the northern end of the Island in the summer.

Most campers that I encounter consider the insects here to be such a trivial problem that they simply ignore them. However I have the uncanny ability to feel bites before they happen, a condition which my wife calls paranoia. I consider it a gift of prescience permitting me to apply liberal doses of deet (a substance which my vegetarian daughter, the entomologist, says is even more dangerous than meat) before the little bastards can disable me.

Alternative approaches are to don protective clothing, or burn a candle scented with citronella, an organically grown substance with a pleasant citrus odour that repels insects.

Methodology

The balance of this book is dedicated to thirty-five of my favourite Island cycling trips. As the following chart indicates, eighteen are routes, and seventeen side routes. They represent a large portion of the Island's inhabited areas. All but those at the remote northern end I have cycled several times, and some many times. All were revisited and documented in the summer of 1995, during which I had to keep reminding myself that I was conducting research, not playing. Alison is still not convinced that riding a bike, camping and drinking beer is work. It was necessary on several occasions to emphasize to her that it was a tough job, and somebody had to do it.

A "route" represents a day's cycle for the average fit rider in reasonably clement weather. Some are circuits; they share a start and end point. Others are linear, starting and ending at different locations. All routes contain the campgrounds at which I typically stay, and the pubs that I frequent. There will often be many other campgrounds en route, usually private. These can be sourced in the annually updated *British Columbia Accommodations* guide, available free at Travel Infocentres. There will usually also be other pubs. Many of these have been documented in *Island Pubbing II* by Robert Moyes (Orca Book Publishers, 1991), available at Island bookstores.

A "side route" extends from a route and usually represents about a half-day's travel, although some are longer. Most are through less inhabited terrain, some are logging roads or unused railway beds. Chosen primarily for their exercise, historic or scenic values, they provide limited services and only the occasional campground or pub.

My maps are intended as guidelines for distances, landmarks, and the locations of camping areas, points of interest and pubs described in the text. For more complete detail I recommend carrying an actual road map.

In addition, for road terrain specifics, for years I've used Simon Priest's *Bicycling Vancouver Island and the Gulf Islands*, included in my bibliography.

Each of the following chapters is dedicated to a single route and, when applicable, its connecting side route(s). Usually one chapter connects with the route of another, facilitating the planning of successive trips. I have used a common format for each chapter. Ostensibly this consistency permits easier reference to the information contained therein. It also made this book a whole lot easier to write.

And for those interested in some of the other methodological minutiae associated with my research:

- distances were measured on the odometers of my car and bicycle, and verified by other relevant documentation.
- the Vancouver Island offices of Human Resource Development Canada assisted tremendously with individual community profiles.
- information on pubs originated from personal and anonymous visits, followed by interviews with their owners. I have no financial interest in any of the pubs in this book. The only money which changed hands was mine, to buy beer and grub. Route chapters contain the addresses and phone numbers of pubs only to assist cyclists in locating them.
- the appended bibliography was supplemented by searches on the Internet, the power of which I'm only beginning to appreciate, and personal interviews. Several of the latter were not conducted inside pubs, and I can actually recall them.

I have enjoyed sharing the experiences and observations of my favourite routes. More importantly, I hope that cycling campers will use this material to begin their own adventures. I recently heard the chief executive officer of a large corporation say that his company values travel experience in potential employees as much as post-secondary training.

The publisher tells me that if this book sells reasonably well over the next few years he will commission an update. Therefore readers' comments, anecdotes and additional relevant information are welcome. And please don't lend copies to friends. Make them buy their own.

Saanich Peninsula

En suivant le genre

I spent the entire summer of 1995 gathering information on my Island routes. When I finally sat down to write about them I had difficulty developing a format. My publisher, Bob Tyrrell, recommended I follow the genre. "Genre" meaning "kind, sort, class, manner," is one of those stylish French words that has insinuated itself into our language because it's more expressive than its English equivalents. For their part, the French probably use "le hot dog" for the same reason.

Anyway, having referenced several texts on travelling the Island, I noted that the format for this genre invariably includes beginning at the Island's south end. While this area has long considered itself the centre of our Island universe, there are also some practical reasons for beginning here. The south Island, population 350,000, has by far the largest concentration of people on the Island. It also attracts the most visitors, the majority of whom arrive via the BC Ferries terminal at Swartz Bay, at the tip of the Saanich Peninsula.

The Saanich Peninsula consists of Central Saanich, North Saanich and Sidney. Central and North Saanich are agricultural and rural residential areas. Greater Victoria's fruits, vegetables and dairy products are produced here. The region has also begun growing specialty products, kiwi fruit being the most notable example. Much of the land has been designated by statute for use exclusively for agricultural purposes. The residential areas are mostly bedroom communities for workers who commute to Greater Victoria. Sidney is the peninsula's commercial centre, primarily a retail sector which caters to tourists and the town's 10,000 residents, most of whose workers also commute to other municipalities.

The Peninsula is well serviced by roads. Highway 17 is a four-lane

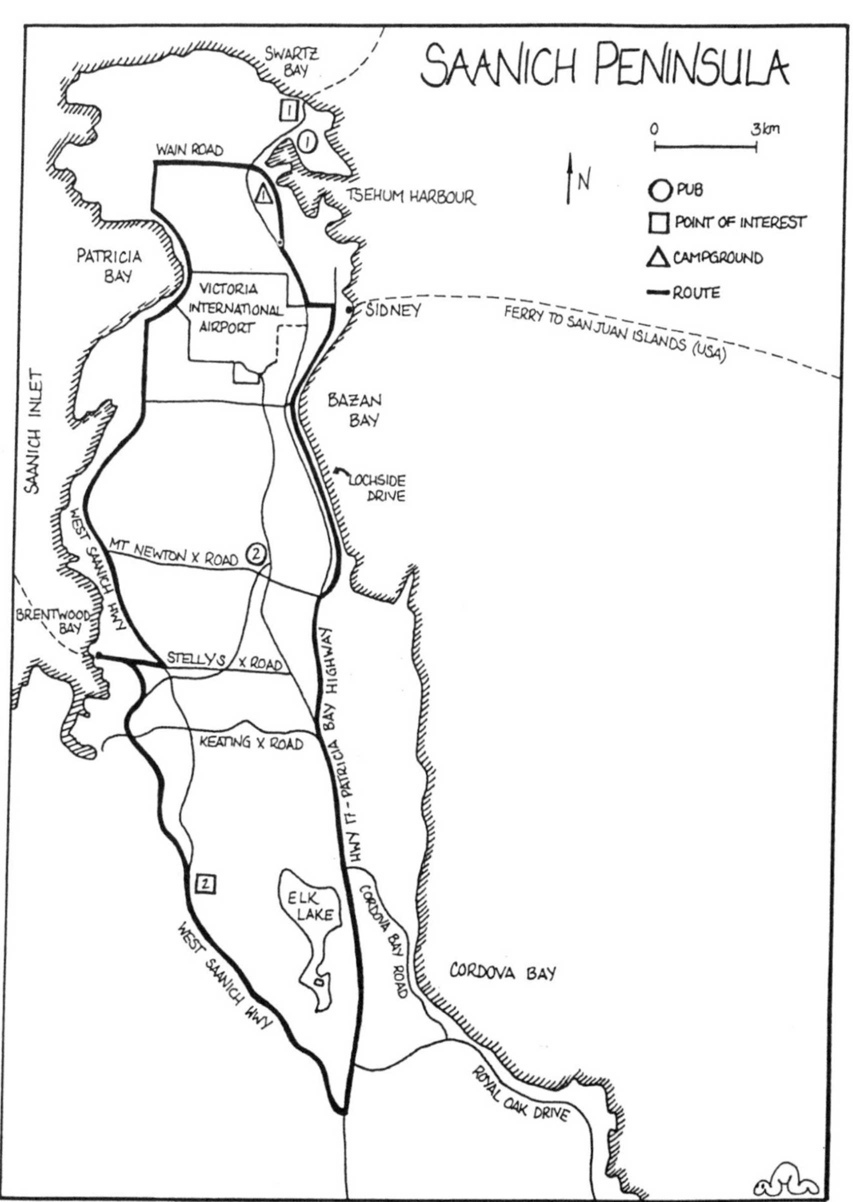

SAANICH PENINSULA
0
3km
N
PUB
POINT OF INTEREST
CAMPGROUND
ROUTE
SWARTZ BAY
1
1
1
WAIN ROAD
TSEHUM HARBOUR
PATRICIA BAY
VICTORIA INTERNATIONAL AIRPORT
SIDNEY
FERRY TO SAN JUAN ISLANDS (USA)
SAANICH INLET
BAZAN BAY
LOCHSIDE DRIVE
WEST SAANICH HWY
MT NEWTON X ROAD
2
BRENTWOOD BAY
STELLYS X ROAD
KEATING X ROAD
HWY 17 - PATRICIA BAY HIGHWAY
2
ELK LAKE
CORDOVA BAY ROAD
CORDOVA BAY
WEST SAANICH HWY
ROYAL OAK DRIVE

route which connects the ferry terminal to Greater Victoria. While always busy with fast-moving vehicles of every sort, the stretch between Elk Lake and Swartz Bay has extremely wide shoulders. I have never felt unsafe here. South of Elk Lake the shoulders narrow, traffic becomes denser, and one encounters a busy series of intersections and overpasses. I advise the timid to leave the route here, and take city streets.

The many other roads which crisscross the area are two lane and tend to be hilly, winding and frequently lacking paved shoulders. However, they are lightly travelled. There is a paved path from the ferry terminal along the east edge of Highway 17 to McDonald Provincial Park, which then links with the roads through Sidney and along Bazan Bay, which is completely flat, a rarity on the Island.

The two pubs that I visit both command superlatives. One is the prettiest I have found on the Island, the other the most diverse.

The subjects of this book are cycling, pubs and camping. But in order to follow the genre, I must begin with a region that possesses great cycling and pubs, but almost no camping. In fact I learned while conducting my research that in spite of increasing demand, the number of campsites in the area is actually shrinking. Non-agricultural land on the Peninsula is scarce and valuable, creating alternative economic opportunities far more rewarding than campgrounds.

Main Route

Road

distance:	50 km; circuit
terrain:	rolling hills; flat from Bazan Bay to ferry terminal
surface:	paved two-lane backroads, narrow or no shoulders; four-lane highway, wide shoulders
traffic:	light to moderate on backroads; heavy to very heavy on highway

Services

bank machines:	Sidney, Swartz Bay ferry terminal, Brentwood Bay
bike repairs:	Sidney
liquor store:	Sidney, Brentwood Bay
groceries:	Sidney, Brentwood Bay
camping:	McDonald Provincial Park, few private campgrounds
hospital:	Central Saanich

My approach

We cycle the Peninsula as a connector between Nanaimo and Victoria, or as a touring destination in itself. As a connector, it avoids the Malahat, a mountainous and heavily travelled highway between Greater Victoria and the Cowichan Valley. There are two options and both involve ferries, either Brentwood Bay/Mill Bay or Swartz Bay/Fulford Harbour. The latter entails travelling the length of Salt Spring Island, and an additional ferry, Crofton/Vesuvius. In either instance, we use the most direct and fastest routes which are West Saanich Rd. and Highway 17 respectively. There are pubs at all terminals except Mill Bay.

The Brentwood Bay/Mill Bay ferry is sometimes removed from service for maintenance and not replaced. Check with BC Ferries to ascertain that it is running. My first experience cycling over the Malahat was a consequence of this oversight.

When touring we base ourselves at McDonald Park. Our most popular route starts with the long flat stretch through Sidney, past Bazan Bay to Mount Newton Cross Road. We then cross the Peninsula to Brentwood Bay. From there Wallace Drive is a flat and quiet ride back to West Saanich Road, which subsequently intersects Highway 17, on which we return to the campground.

It is also possible to tour Victoria from this campground and return in a day, provided one does not plan extended visits to that city's attractions. In addition to being a good workout, camping at McDonald Park leaves the cyclist well positioned to take either of the aforementioned ferries the next day.

Swartz Bay Ferry Terminal (PI1)

Of the two major ferry terminals on the Island (the other is in Nanaimo), this is the larger. It connects the mainland with the lower Island, and also serves the Gulf Islands. Its docks process more than thirty vessel arrivals and departures a day, totaling 7.5 million passengers and nearly three million vehicles annually.

The two new prides of the fleet, the Spirits of British Columbia and Vancouver Island, serve the Swartz Bay/Tsawwassen route. These 168 m (550 ft) giants carry 470 vehicles and 2100 passengers at a speed of 19.5 knots (36 kph).

While the terminal is busy and complex, effective signage and helpful shore personnel make it easy and safe for cyclists to enter and leave.

Stonehouse Pub on the Saanich Peninsula

The Stonehouse Pub (Pub1)

2215 Canoe Cove Road (656-3498)

The Stonehouse Pub, located near the entrance to the ferry terminal, is the prettiest pub on the Island. Built in 1932, it was a private residence until 1985. Constructed from hand-cut stone, the pub occupies a hectare of flower gardens and forest, on the edge of Tsehum Harbour.

Its decor is "very English," and fittingly it serves ten brands of premium draft, including two Irish and two English. This is a quiet pub. It caters to the over-forty crowd. There are no TVs, and the background music is either light jazz or classical.

McDonald Provincial Park (CG1)

30 sites

This quiet, heavily treed campground is close to the Swartz Bay ferry terminal and the town of Sidney. We use it as a layover before catching the ferries from either of these locations, or as a base from which to explore the Peninsula. When I last visited, the nearby yacht club allowed campers to use its coin-operated showers. We have always found a vacant spot at McDonald, but the staff at the Infocentre recently advised me that it fills rapidly in the summer, usually with RVs, as a result of the general shortage of campsites in the area.

Sidney

As indicated earlier, the town of Sidney, population ten thousand, is predominantly a pleasant residential and retail centre. It is also home to two ferry docks. A small passenger ferry transports campers and sightseers to Sidney Spit Marine Park (thirty sites) on the tip of nearby Sidney Island. The park, which has a beautiful beach, is a popular spot for young people and can get rowdy at night.

A second terminal receives the Washington State Ferry to the San Juan Islands, another excellent touring destination for cycling campers.

The Prairie Inn (Pub2)

7806 East Saanich Road (652-1575)

The Prairie Inn is more than a pub, it's a complex that includes the pub's three separate rooms in addition to a brewery and a "boutique-style Beer and Wine Emporium."

The pub is housed in a distinctive two-storey building that was built as a hotel in 1893. In 1974 the Inn became Vancouver Island's first neighbourhood pub (a distinction also claimed by the Crow and Gate in Nanaimo). In 1983 it was for a while the Island's only brewery, by producing its own lagers in an adjoining cottage. One of the unique features of the 600 gallon per week brewery is the refrigerated underground direct beer link between the brewery and the taps in the pub. This direct draw system was the first of its kind in Canada, and to become legal required a change in the federal government's Excise Liquor Act.

The pub features a quiet room and a sports bar (eighteen TVs), and art provided by a local gallery.

Dominion Astrophysical Observatory (PI2)

My first time past the entrance to this facility, I was tempted to ignore it. Big telescopes are no big deal to someone who has lived in Toronto, where they are abundant. Besides, the observatory looked like it might be at the top of a pretty big hill. It was. As it happened, the 2 km driveway rose 200 m. It was worth it for the view alone which looked west across the Saanich Inlet, and over the peaks of Vancouver Island's mountains.

The observatory was constructed in 1918 and has been continuously up-dated since. Its huge telescope collects and focuses light from the planets, stars and galaxies. A spectrograph separates the light into its component colours which are then analyzed to determine distance, age, size, velocity and other characteristics. This observatory is among the world leaders in studying the universe.

The telescope's original mirror is displayed here. It is 1.8 m (72") in diameter, and weighs 1972 kg (4348 lb). It took four years to grind to its desired specifications.

Side Route — San Juan Islands

distance:	50 – 65 km per island; circuits
terrain:	winding roads, rolling hills
surface:	paved two lane, mostly without shoulders
traffic:	light

While close geographically to the Gulf Islands, the American San Juan Islands are a world apart. In addition to the cultural contrast, they exhibit different vegetation due to lower annual rainfall, and less standing forest as a result of a longer established population.

The three islands most popular to cyclists are San Juan, Orcas and Lopez. I recommend spending a day on each. San Juan has at each end the historic sites of English and American camps, antagonists in the thirteen year non-combative Pig War over the boundary between the USA and Canada. Friday Harbor is a lively port community full of boutiques and taverns. Orcas has some great hills, including Mount Constitution, a 735 m peak with a breathtaking 360° view. Conveniently having the excuse of view-restricting low cloud cover on my only visit to Orcas, I have not yet cycled the road to this peak, which I'm told is a challenge. Lopez bills itself as "A Bicyclist's Paradise." It's not as hilly as the other islands, has less traffic, and has a beautiful waterfront campground, Spencer Spit State Park.

Information on the San Juans is available at the Sidney Travel Infocentre and on the Washington State Ferries. This information includes campsites, which are limited, so I recommend reserving ahead. The ferry to the San Juans leaves Sidney twice a day in the summer, and once the rest of the year. Arrive early in order to clear customs.

A regular rider of BC ferries will immediately notice that Washington State ferries are different. While BC ferries are punctual almost to a fault, Washington State ferries appear to regard their schedules more as suggestions than a rigid timetable. In my experience these ferries rarely arrive or depart on time. And, Washington State ferries serve beer.

One more note on Washington State ferries — check the expiry date of your schedule, which changes more frequently than just summer and winter. We learned this the hard way one July when it changed in the middle of a two-day trip. We had to break camp at 4:30 A.M. in order to catch a connecting route to the only ferry of the day sailing back to Sidney.

Side Route(s) — Saanich Peninsula Backroads

What follows is a departure from both the revered genre and my format in subsequent chapters. As I indicated earlier, the peninsula is crisscrossed with backroads, and all are excellent for cycling. There are too many possible variations to list each as an individual side route.

However on my last visit to the Sidney Infocentre I acquired a brochure entitled "Cycling and Souvenir Map of the Saanich Peninsula." Also available at the Sidney bike store, this details ten Peninsula cycling routes all originating and ending in Sidney. They vary in distance from 10 to 35 km, and estimated times from 45 minutes to 3.5 hours. Destinations include beaches, farms, a mountain, and even a fitness facility with a squash court. In addition Laurel McIntyre, the owner of City Scribe Printing and Stationery (fax 652-6173) which produced the brochure, has kindly agreed to provide a copy upon request.

Greater Victoria

The Immaculate Deception

Although this chapter appears as the second (the dreaded "genre" again) in my series of routes, I wrote it last. My delay emanated from an ambivalence I have always felt about Victoria. Most people I know fall in love with this city on the first visit. To many, its sophisticated, manicured beauty and prosperous colonial charm are irresistible. However, this tweedy, well-preserved seductress is still a city, and to me embodies the noise, traffic, odours, lineups and other urban accoutrements from which I moved to the Island to escape. Besides, my book's theme of cycling and camping is hardly compatible with a mini-metropolis of 290,000.

Greater Victoria is comprised of four municipalities, Victoria, Oak Bay, Esquimalt and Saanich. Although they abut, each is distinctly different. Victoria is the provincial capital and the Island's largest commercial centre and tourist attraction. Oak Bay, "behind the tweed curtain," is an established shoreline residential area that contains some of the most desirable and expensive homes in Canada. Saanich is a sprawling suburb of middle-class residences, small businesses and strip malls. And Esquimalt is a working man's town — an industrial district, and home to dockyards and a naval base.

The cycling visitor should heed two cautions. First, while the area's drivers are courteous and its streets wide, the streets often lack shoulders, are frequently hilly and winding, and always busy. Secondly, like any city this one also has its share of thieves. It is not uncommon to see cyclists walking through town, seat posts in hand. Their mounts have not been stolen from beneath them. They simply can't leave even a locked bike unattended and expect anything that isn't bolted on to be there

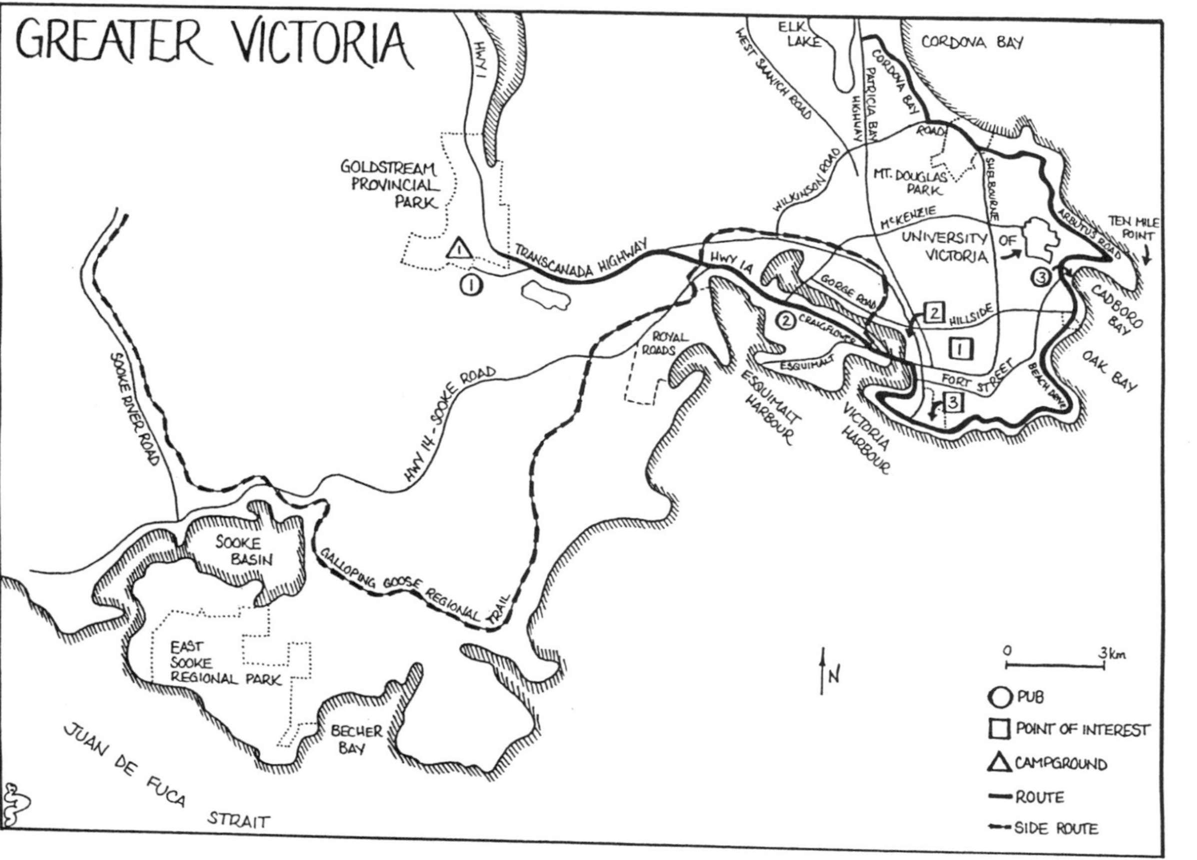
GREATER VICTORIA
HWY 1
GOLDSTREAM PROVINCIAL PARK
TRANSCANADA HIGHWAY
ELK LAKE
WEST SAANICH ROAD
PATRICIA BAY HIGHWAY
CORDOVA BAY ROAD
CORDOVA BAY
WILKINSON ROAD
MT. DOUGLAS PARK
SHELBOURNE
McKENZIE
UNIVERSITY OF VICTORIA
ARBUTUS ROAD
TEN MILE POINT
CADBORO BAY
OAK BAY
BEACH DRIVE
HWY 1A
GORGE ROAD
CRAIGFLOWER
HILLSIDE
ESQUIMALT
FORT STREET
ESQUIMALT HARBOUR
VICTORIA HARBOUR
ROYAL ROADS
SOOKE RIVER ROAD
HWY 14 - SOOKE ROAD
SOOKE BASIN
GALLOPING GOOSE REGIONAL TRAIL
EAST SOOKE REGIONAL PARK
BECHER BAY
JUAN DE FUCA STRAIT
N
0
3km
PUB
POINT OF INTEREST
CAMPGROUND
ROUTE
SIDE ROUTE

when they return.

As a map of Victoria reveals, there are innumerable routes through it. My choice follows the ocean front perimeter of Greater Victoria. It includes the Inner Harbour and downtown of Victoria, passes the shipyards and naval base in Esquimalt, and skirts the quiet and affluent residential districts of Oak Bay and the Uplands. The cyclist can absorb the ambience this city promotes so well, without being distracted by excessive traffic. Depending on direction of travel, it is also a scenic connector to the Saanich Peninsula, Island Highway and the west coast road to Port Renfrew.

There is no tenting within the area. The closest sites are on the Saanich Peninsula. After leaving Victoria on the Island Highway, there is a private campground near Thetis Lake, followed by Goldstream Provincial Park.

Partly because of its British influence, Victoria has oodles of pubs. While the three mentioned in this chapter are directly en route, there are others both on the route and near it.

Note: The Greater Victoria Cycling Coalition (GVCC), an advocacy group for cyclists in the area, produces a map of cycling routes which designates light and heavy traffic commuter routes, touring and recreation routes, and trails and gravel roads. I recommend this to cyclists planning extensive travel in the area. It is available at Infocentres, bike stores, or from the GVCC, 1275 Oscar St., Victoria, BC, V8V 2X6 (phone 381-2453).

MAIN ROUTE

Road

distance:	55 km (one way); linear
terrain:	winding, rolling hills and flat stretches
surface:	paved streets, mostly four lane; narrow or no shoulders
traffic:	moderate to heavy

Services

bank machines:	numerous banks and businesses in each municipality
bike repairs:	several in each municipality
liquor store:	several in each municipality
groceries:	many large and small stores
camping:	outlying municipalities only
hospital:	Victoria

My approach

When based at Goldstream Provincial Park this return route is a scenic one-day tour of Victoria's waterfront and downtown. The route passes through a number of shoreline parks, all excellent spots for a break or picnic. The route can also be transformed to a circuit, and shortened by following city streets through Saanich. This entails exposure to denser traffic.

One could easily spend an entire day exploring the Inner Harbour area, with its collection of wharves, historic buidings and attractions, stores and eateries, all of which can be toured by foot. I try to find a sympathetic business that will let me store my bike while doing this.

I also take the route when cycling between downtown and the ferry terminal at Swartz Bay. It takes a little longer but the scenery is worth it.

I camp at Goldstream Provincial Park, which is a destination in itself, and accessible to the Galloping Goose trail, a must for any cyclist touring the region.

A brief history of Victoria

Victoria was founded in 1843 as Fort Victoria, a Hudson's Bay Company outpost and an unsuccessful attempt to avoid the encroachment of settlers on its fur trading operations. The colony grew rapidly, affected by a series of external events. After Britain concluded her treaty with the USA in 1846 that established the border with British North America, Victoria became a strategic outpost and port of entry to Britain's most western colony. The Crimean War between Britain and Russia motivated the construction of the Royal Navy Base at Esquimalt as a port for the British fleet. The colony later became a new home for refugees from the American Civil War, and a supply and transportation point for thousands of gold seekers travelling to the Fraser Gold Rush.

The British influence was begun and continued by that country's administrators, civil servants and naval officers, to whom England was a spiritual home. Determined to preserve their heritage, parks and gardens were created in the fashion of their homeland, and streets and buildings were designed as sources of civic pride.

Today Victoria is one of the west coast's most desirable destinations to work, retire, or holiday. It has an aura which combines a reverence for history with a tidy sense of "Britishness," nestled under a gossamer of affluence. The city has often been dubbed more British than the British, flaunting double decker buses, union jacks, tweed sports coats and that generally supercilious air often donned by cultures that equate appearance with substance.

Its substance derives primarily from three activities: growing old, showing off and spending tax dollars. Statistics reveal that Victoria performs all three well. Almost since its founding it has been a popular home for retirees. Today 30 percent of its population is age fifty-five or over.

The number of tourists, which increases annually, was 3.5 million in 1994. This contributes significantly to employment in the accommodation, food and beverage, and retail sectors, which employ one worker in five.

Currently 37 percent (52,000) of the area's total workforce of 139,000 thousand are public servants involved in government, education or health and social services. The federal and provincial governments alone employ over twenty-two thousand. Of the twenty largest employers, eighteen are in the public sector.

Goldstream Provincial Park (CG1)

150 sites, washrooms, showers, swimming, reservations permitted

Goldstream was donated in 1958 to the province by the Greater Victoria Water Board, whose watershed borders the park. In addition to being an excellent camping area, it's a great spot to explore. The park is nearly 4 km long and contains an estimated 10 km of trails. Sights include six-hundred-year-old trees, a 47.5 m waterfall, the old shafts and tunnels of some short-lived 1850s gold mining activity, and a spectacular fall salmon spawning migration.

The park is a practical base from which to tour Victoria, and a convenient stopover when having completed or about to begin the Malahat. Always busy and full in the summer. While there is no designated hiker/biker area, the park staff assured me that they would find a spot for a needy tenter, even if it's in the overflow parking lot.

Ma Miller's Goldstream Inn (Pub1)

2903 Sooke Lake Road (478-3512)

Even if Ma Miller's was not fortuitously located at the entrance to Goldstream Park, it would still be unique. It is the oldest continuously licensed establishment in BC and one of a series of former stagecoach stops in the area that are now pubs.

The pub's owners maintain a strong commitment to the surrounding community. Pub-sponsored charity events distribute thousands of dollars annually into the surrounding area. During a recent prolonged winter power failure the pub suspended serving alcohol in order to provide a warm haven for neighbouring families.

I experienced this largesse firsthand during a visit on "two-for-one steak night." I sat next to a retired gentleman enjoying his steak dinner alone. During our chat he volunteered that because he was a widower and only a "one," Ma Miller's provided his meal for half price. I have since learned that the pub extends this policy to all customers of similar status.

Tudor House Pub (Pub2)

533 Admirals Road (382-5625)

The Tudor House is in Esquimalt, where the working folk live. A few short blocks after leaving downtown Victoria the average age drops twenty years and pick-ups replace Jaguar sedans. The Tudor House Pub, which seats 217, was built in 1904 as a home for retired seamen. It acquired pub status in 1937, and is still visited regularly by a gentleman who began to drink there at about that time.

The pub leaves the impression of beig stuck in an identity crisis. It has been recently renovated as a "sports bar," and one large area is dedicated to TVs, pool tables and pictures of athletes. The other side is lead glass windows, brass and oak, and arborite. The pub's name, depending on whether you look at the logo on the carpet or the bar, is either Tudor House or Port of Call. The owners had also tried to change it to Jocks and Jills, but relented in the face of outrage by the regulars. Somehow it all works. This is a very happy pub.

Victoria Inner Harbour and Downtown (PI1)

When I think of Victoria, my mind pictures this area. Many of the city's perfectly preserved and nurtured heritage sites and buildings can be absorbed from here.

The Inner Harbour was once moorage for all incoming commerce and passengers into city, and continues to be the centrepiece and hub of the downtown. In summer hundreds of visiting pleasure boats tie up here and can be viewed from a walkway which circles it. The stores and eateries of downtown are easily accessible by foot from here.

The three attractions that follow are only the most visible. There are many others, and I recommend that the visiting history buff acquire a guide to them from an Infocentre.

Royal British Columbia Museum

Recognized as one of the best museums in the world, the Royal BC Museum was first built in 1886 and now hosts one million visitors a year. Actually, one doesn't visit this museum, one is absorbed by it. Displays include a turn of the century town, mine and farm, and forest, sea shore and undersea exhibits. They register on all the senses. An exhibit of an old hotel kitchen includes the smell of baking apple pie.

The ticket to the undersea exhibit, a simulated bathysphere trip to the ocean bottom which goes awry, includes a warning "If you suffer from claustrophobia we ask that you not enter this exhibit."

Empress Hotel

The Empress, one of the world-famous CPR chateaux, was completed in 1908 after four years of construction. Because its site was formerly tidal flats, it was built on hundreds of deeply driven wooden piles. The hotel is rumoured to sink a centimeter or two every decade.

Over the years it has hosted the rich and famous, but is remembered by millions as the site of afternoon tea, a quaint British custom which serves 100,000 visitors a year, and for which one must book in advance. This practice, begun when Victoria was a booming port occupied with other forms of commerce, is thought to be the original basis of the city's tourism industry.

Provincial Legislature

The visitor will be excused for confusing the Legislature with the Empress. They are both enormous edifices, and they were designed by the same architect, a then-young Francis Rattenbury. Rattenbury went on to design other notable homes and buildings in area.

At night the Legislature is lit by thirty-three hundred bulbs, a tradition which began in 1897 to celebrate Queen Victoria's Diamond Jubilee.

Vancouver Island Brewery (PI2)

While researching this book I realized that the term "micro-brewery" had crept into my vocabulary without my really knowing what one was. To me it connoted large copper kettles being tended in dark, backrooms by stout, balding men with aprons and German accents. Their product, while meticulously tended would be inconsistent in flavour due to unsophisticated methods. While ruminating over how to create a tour of Victoria for readers of this book that would differ from standard tourist fare, I learned that Vancouver Island Brewery, a micro-brewer, had just opened a new facility on the edge of downtown Victoria (2230 Government Street).

I visited this brewery with a buddy, and we were fortunate to have been taken on a personal tour by the brewmaster, Ross Elliot. Ross is neither stout nor balding, nor does he wear an apron or sound in the least Teutonic. He was educated in his profession at an American university, followed by experience in European breweries. His tour then dissolved the rest of my misconceptions.

While committed to the hands-on production of quality, specialty brews, micro-breweries are in fact defined by their output. Their annual volume cannot exceed 7.5 million litres per year. Micro-breweries currently account for about six percent of all Canadian beer production, and their output is increasing at an annual rate of 25 percent. Vancouver Island Breweries currently produces about 1.5 million litres in a state-of-the-art facility that boasts all stainless steel equipment, a meticulously controlled germ-free environment, and computerized monitoring systems so sophisticated that they can call Ross at home at night, from where he can also control the brewing process.

The brewery welcomes visitors and conducts tours twice a day. A tour ends with a visit to a hospitality room where guests can sample the company's beers.

Beacon Hill Park (PI3)

Beacon Hill Park, on the edge of downtown, was designed in the British manner as a centre for family activity. Its acres include playing fields, gardens, and a wildfowl sanctuary complete with swans. While well served by a network of quiet, paved roads, the trail along the ocean is off-limits to cyclists.

A post which designates Mile Zero of the Trans-Canada Highway is located at the park's southwest corner, a symbolic attraction for any cyclist planning to travel the length of Vancouver Island.

The Cock and Bull (Pub3)

2581 Penrhyn Street (477-2688)

The Cock and Bull is one of those instant "Ye Olde Pub" structures that actually pulls it off. The pub is on two levels, with most of the seating being upstairs. Its interior is all angles, and nooks and wood beams and feels very conspiratorial. When I have visited it has been quiet, its customers being either retirees or students from the nearby University of Victoria, noses in books. An interior sign requests that patrons refrain from "brown bagging."

Here I was exposed to a novel marketing technique that I have seen neither before or since. While glancing at a televised football game a graphic showed that the Raiders were leading the Bengals 20 to 3. They had amassed 270 total yards of offence to the Bengals' 145, and wings were 15¢ on Mondays. The pub uses an electronic device which records promotional messages and transmits them via cable to its televisions.

The pub sells ten types of draft beer, and features the products of micro-breweries.

Side Route — Galloping Goose Regional Trail

distance:	47 km; linear
terrain:	extended flat stretches
surface:	abandoned railway bed, trestles
traffic:	other cyclists, hikers and horses; vehicles prohibited

The Galloping Goose was our introduction to cycling on abandoned railway beds, a pastime we now pursue as a hobby. There are many such sites on the Island, but none as well preserved as this.

The Goose is a regional park and is also the first rails-to-trails conversion in Canada, a project intended to link rail beds across the country, enabling users to travel from coast to coast to coast (a connector to the Arctic is also envisaged).

The Goose begins at View Royal, a suburb on the edge of Victoria, and winds through suburbs, along the Sooke basin, and follows the Sooke River to Leechtown. This community, a former mining town, exists now only as a large clearing overgrown with broom, its buildings having been demolished to frustrate the efforts of vandals. We were also advised that the mines near Leechtown are open and serve as dens for cougars. Cougar sightings are common in the area.

There are some high trestles en route which have recently been boarded over and fenced for the safety of users.

My dominant memory of the route relates to a structure we encountered just north of Sooke Potholes Provincial Park. At first we thought it was a derelict building but then realized that it was an immense unfinished wooden building commanding a magnificent view of the Sooke Canyon. We have since been told that its builder encountered financial difficulties and simply abandoned the project. It has a roof, is framed for walls and contains several fire places, one so large that a group was camped around a fire they had lit in it.

A map of the trail is available from Infocentres in the area, or from the Capital Regional District Park office.

Salt Spring Island

So, you enjoy hills?

When I first entertained writing this book, this was the route that came to mind. I have cycled it countless times, alone and with friends, at all times of the year and it still keeps drawing me back. It has some hills guaranteed to work up a thirst, a unique town (Ganges), several spectacular views, and my all-time favourite campground, Ruckle Provincial Park.

The routes, while not particularly long (combined, they can be covered in two days), are challenging. On Salt Spring the cyclist is either going up or coming down. There are very few level stretches, and some of the hills are real beauties. Traffic is light, except in Ganges and at the ferry terminals directly before and after loadings. Motorists occasionally get a little frustrated with cyclists, a consequence of narrow winding roads and narrow or non-existent shoulders.

Main Route

Road

distance:	55 km; circuit
terrain:	rolling hills, some steep
surface:	paved, two-lane; narrow or no shoulders
traffic:	light to moderate

Services

bank machine:	Ganges (several)
bike repairs:	Ganges

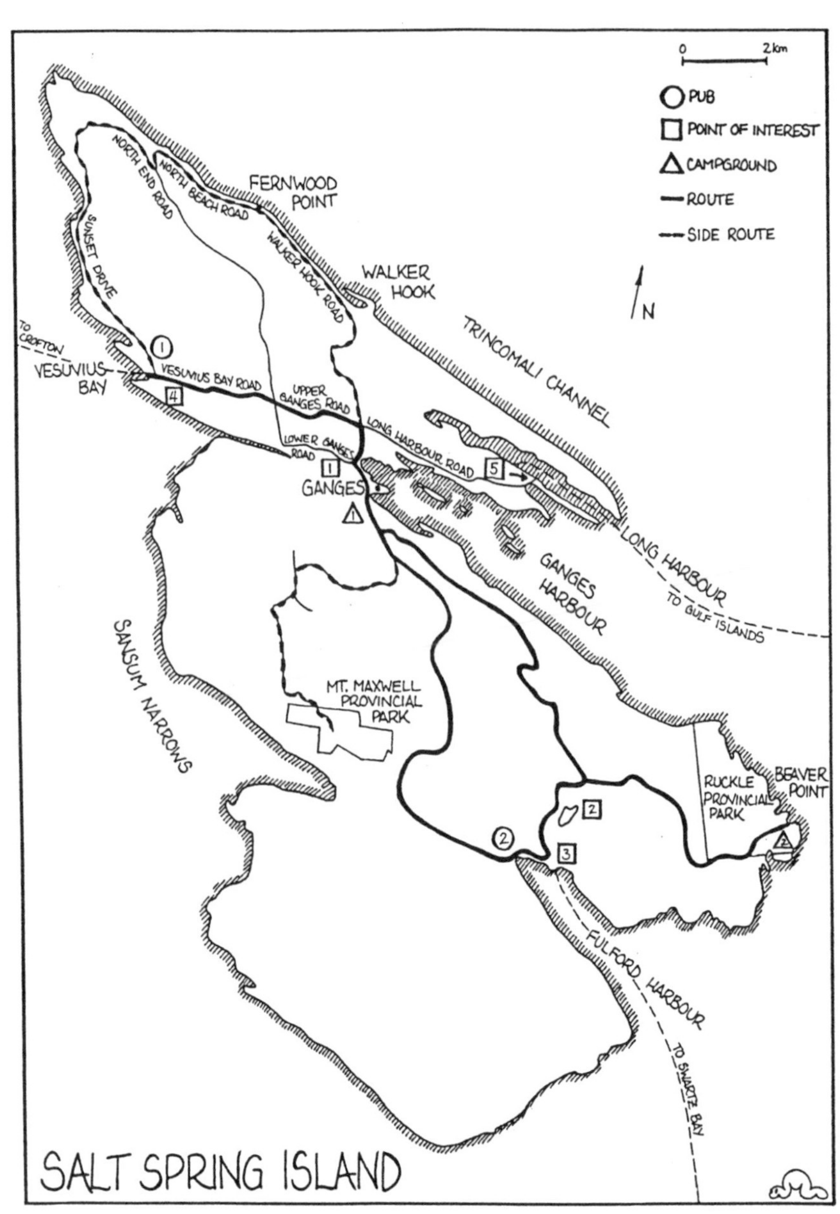

0
2 km
PUB
POINT OF INTEREST
CAMPGROUND
ROUTE
SIDE ROUTE
N
NORTH END ROAD
NORTH BEACH ROAD
FERNWOOD POINT
SUNSET DRIVE
WALKER HOOK ROAD
WALKER HOOK
TRINCOMALI CHANNEL
TO CROFTON
VESUVIUS BAY
VESUVIUS BAY ROAD
UPPER GANGES ROAD
LONG HARBOUR ROAD
LOWER GANGES ROAD
GANGES
LONG HARBOUR
TO GULF ISLANDS
GANGES HARBOUR
SANSUM NARROWS
MT. MAXWELL PROVINCIAL PARK
RUCKLE PROVINCIAL PARK
BEAVER POINT
FULFORD HARBOUR
TO SWARTZ BAY
SALT SPRING ISLAND

groceries:	Ganges, Fulford Harbour
liquor store:	Ganges
hospital:	Ganges
camping:	Ruckle and Mouat provincial parks, private sites (mostly around St. Mary Lake)

Ferry access to Salt Spring

Salt Spring Island is accessed by ferry at three points. There is a ferry from Tsawwassen on the mainland which docks at Long Harbour, after connecting with some of the other Gulf Islands. This route is very popular with cyclists from Vancouver because it eliminates having to disembark first at Vancouver Island and then board another ferry to Salt Spring. Daily sailings are scheduled but infrequent, and the traveller is advised to consult a timetable rather than be disappointed by a very long wait.

The other two points are reached from Vancouver Island. The ferry to Vesuvius at the north end of Salt Spring is boarded at Crofton. Fulford Harbour, at the south end is reached from Swartz Bay. While scheduled, both these runs are short, a half hour or so, so we seldom aim for a particular time. There'll be another sailing in an hour and there are great pubs at both ends of each route.

Sometimes at Swartz Bay the disembarking cyclist from the mainland can roll straight onto the Fulford Harbour ferry, saving the inconvenience of having to return to the toll booth and re-enter. The ferry shore personnel who direct traffic can be most helpful with this procedure, which is a major time saver, if asked. Just remember to say that you will pay the purser when aboard. This also works when returning from Salt Spring.

My approach

We frequently begin this route at Vesuvius, and make Ganges our first stop, usually for groceries and other essentials. Leaving Ganges for Fulford Harbour is an uphill whose only redemption is its equivalent downhill into Fulford Harbour and the Fulford Inn. Leaving Fulford is another steep hill, also with a corresponding downhill several kilometres later into Ruckle Park. We overnight at Ruckle, returning by way of Stewart Road, and another pretty fair hill. However this is a change of scenery and shortens the route by a few kilometres. Once in Ganges, depending on our schedule we either shop and sightsee, or go directly to Vesuvius, where we can wait in the Vesuvius Inn for the ferry to Crofton.

When travelling from Victoria or Swartz Bay I frequently use Salt Spring as a shortcut to my home in Nanaimo. It's much shorter and avoids the dreaded Malahat Drive.

A brief history of Salt Spring Island.

Salt Spring is the largest of the Gulf Islands. It is believed to have been a summer home for the early Native communities due to its warm, dry climate and abundance of sealife. It derives its name from a formation of brine pools near St. Mary Lake.

Encouraged by land at one dollar an acre, settlers began to arrive in the 1860s mostly to farm. For a while Salt Spring was major producer of lamb, fruits and dairy products for the colony of Vancouver Island and other destinations. Farming continues to be a significant economic activity, as is tourism. The island also boasts a large and active arts and crafts community, some of whose works are known internationally.

Vesuvius Inn (Pub1)

The Vesuvius Inn is located at the top of the ferry dock. It is the largest landmark in the village, a grand old building whose architecture to me vaguely resembles the ante-bellum South. On entering, one is immediately aware of two features — its expanse of polished oak floors, and the view from nearly every table across Stuart Channel to Crofton on Vancouver Island. Another feature, not quite so obvious but important to me, is that in this pub one can always find a current newspaper, thereby gaining when necessary a temporary distraction from one's travelling companions.

There is a strong emphasis on variety of menu and timelines of service. The food here is always exceptional, and one can actually eat healthily should one be perverse enough to wish to do so. The timeliness may be necessitated by having to serve a clientele that is frequently waiting to catch a ferry, whose arrivals and departures can be monitored through the pub windows.

Ganges (PI1)

Ganges is the main population centre on the island. This community of 8,000 has a vibrant year-round downtown district which includes all the basic services needed by cyclists, plus some specialty food, clothing and art boutiques. All are within easy walking distance of each other. On Saturday mornings the park at the centre of town hosts a marketplace in which local artisans show and sell their products.

There is a row of stores before ascending the hill which includes a bakery, deli, and a specialty coffee and chocolate shop. Alison finds it impossible not to visit these and her purchases make nice treats later at the campsite.

Mouat Provincial Park (CG1)

15 sites

The chief asset of Mouat is its proximity to Ganges, which can be accessed on a bike by a short downhill coast.

Because it is a small campground, it is frequently full during the tourist season. In several attempts during this period I have yet to succeed in getting a spot. However we have found it to be a delightfully private place during the off-season, when there are few other campers, or when it is closed for the winter. At this time the entrance is barred by a barrier that can be circumvented only by hikers and cyclists. Although there are no services at this time, the custodian appears to have no objection to our staying there. During such negotiations I find it helpful to extend a trembling lower lip, as taught by my buddy Moddle.

Fulford Harbour Inn (Pub2)

On a hot day, having just cycled across the top of Salt Spring from Ganges, the Fulford Inn appears like a Tudor oasis. It is the lone building at the end of the harbour, the entire length of which one can see through the pub's windows. It is the last watering hole before Ruckle Park.

We have been stopping there for years, through several successive ownerships. Quite frankly, although always a welcome and friendly spot, it was starting to look a little run-down. That was changing when I visited for my research. The pub had been purchased several months previously by Alf Reda, to whom I introduced myself by carelessly destroying one of his new hanging flower baskets with my head.

For several weeks Al had a crew of carpenters working at nights, after closing, to completely refurbish and redecorate the pub in an oak and brass motif. This work will now have been completed.

We often sit there longer than we should, knowing that it is our last stop before Ruckle Park, and there is a major hill to be conquered immediately on leaving. It is also a great spot to watch for the arrival of the ferry from Swartz Bay, which docks about a ten-minute ride away.

Ruckle Provincial Park (CG2)

70 sites, handpump for water

At 486 hectares, Ruckle is the largest provincial park in the Gulf Islands. Located on Beaver Point it was homesteaded in 1872 by Henry Ruckle. At the turn of the century this farm was producing cattle, sheep, pigs, turkeys, wheat, oats, hay, vegetables and fruit. In 1977 the Ruckle family sold the farm for a nominal amount to the provincial government on the condition it be used as a park.

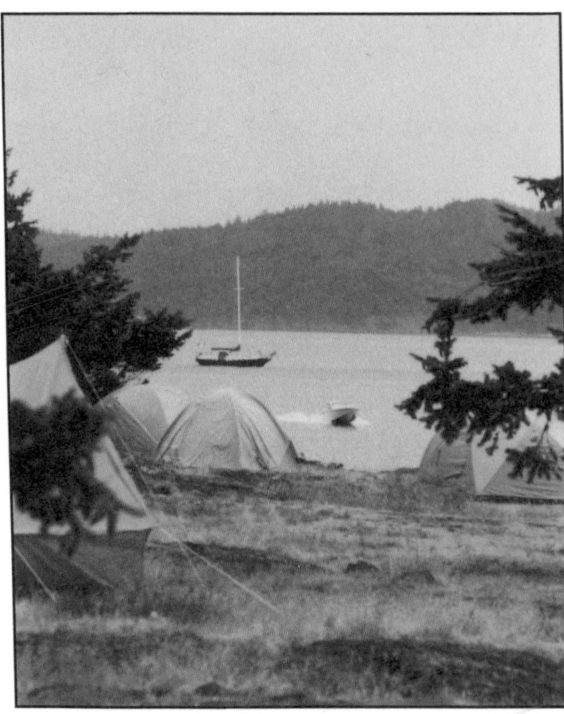

Ruckle Provincial Park, "the tent village"

Part of the property is still actively farmed. Many of the old buildings are being restored for viewing.

Camping is on Beaver Point, a huge grassy area of shoreline with a view south to the American San Juan Islands. The sites are accessible only by foot or on bike. Well water is available from two handpumps, one at the centre of the campground, the other in the parking lot above. We have found the latter to be a better choice. During prolonged dry spells water from the campground pump can be a little discoloured and odorous, and should be boiled before drinking.

When staying at Ruckle, be prepared to spend a lot of time just looking out from shore. The already spectacular view is augmented by the frequent passing of BC ferries, seals and sea lions, and the occasional whale and porpoise. Remember to close food packs securely at night; raccoons abound. It was at Ruckle that a mink entered our pack and bored down the length of a French loaf.

Tip: during the summer this campground will often be marked "Full." While there are no specifically designated tent sites in this huge park, there are only seventy picnic tables distributed across it. A full campground means the tables have all been rented. It is still possible to share the cost of a table with its renter, and pitch a tent at a sufficient distance to maintain privacy.

Miscellaneous points of interest

- Stowell Lake (P12) — fresh-water swimming, raft, portable toilets.
- Fulford Harbour ferry dock (P13) — deli, general store, groceries.
- Vesuvius (P14) — store, deli.
- Long Harbour ferry dock (P15) — ferry to mainland and other Gulf Islands. Galiano, Mayne and the Penders offer excellent cycling.

Side Route — Mount Maxwell Provincial Park

distance:	9 km; linear
terrain:	uphill to the peak
surface:	paved, two lane with no shoulders, followed by gravel surface, sometimes soft
traffic:	very light
rest area:	at the peak

This route, the entrance to which is well marked, is begun near the top of the hill leaving Ganges on the road to Fulford Harbour. It is not a trip for the faint of heart, being 9 km of only partly paved road to an altitude of 594 m at Baynes Peak, the highest point on Salt Spring Island.

We first tackled this early one morning after camping at Mouat. The reasons are only now becoming clear to me. Our companions, Terry and Judy, are both obsessive/compulsive, so they had to do it because it was there. And Alison enjoys any activity that makes me suffer. And first thing in the morning I'm too dozy to say "no."

These are my dimly held recollections of the route:

- up, up, and more up
- perspiration
- lightening the bikes, so they wouldn't sink into the gravel, by removing our gear and hiding it in the bushes
- the superb view from the peak
- a very quick return route

There is an expansive treed picnic area and extended lookout at the peak with a view of Vancouver Island and some of the other Gulf Islands.

From one vantage point you will see the road into Fulford Harbour, a destination which is a half hour to an hour away by cycle.

SIDE ROUTE — THE NORTH CIRCUIT

distance:	25 km; circuit
terrain:	rolling hills, some steep
surface:	paved, two lane; narrow or no shoulders
traffic:	light

If you are camping at Mouat Park and plan to spend a half day or so exploring Ganges, this route is an excellent workout combined with an opportunity to view the lesser travelled end of the island.

We first toured it while boating. We carried our bikes with us to assist in gaining a more complete perspective on the places which we visited, plus get some excercise. Traffic is light, offering ample opportunity to ride side-by-side and chat, with the scenery mostly homes, cottages and farms. During the spring the fields are filled with wild daffodils. I have one dominant memory of this route — that of a young lamb sucking milk contentedly from a cow, which was presumably its surrogate mother.

The road past Fernwood has flat stretches and is close to shore, with views of Trincomali Channel and Galiano Island.

The Cowichan Valley Wine Road

As if pubs weren't enough!

Even though it is only 60 km from my home, I learned about the Wine Road only by accident. While conducting some reasearch for my day job I met one of the winery owners. She informed me of the existence of the wineries, and a recent tourism initiative to promote the route connecting them.

The route winds through mostly rolling hills and farmland, avoiding all but a short stretch of the Island Highway. The wineries, and one ciderworks, are connected by comfortable cycling distances. The only notable steep hill is encountered when leaving the village of Cowichan Bay from the south. The route also passes through four population centres, Mill Bay, Cobble Hill, Cowichan Bay and the city of Duncan.

The Wine Road is very special to me. It is an educational experience and an opportunity to meet some truly unique people. And it launched my writing career. Alison and I first cycled the route one clear February weekend, and our observations became the topic of my first magazine article.

Main Route

Road

distance:	76 km; circuit
terrain:	rolling hills, flat stretches
surface:	paved, two-lane, narrow or no shoulders; short tretch of four-lane, wide shoulders
traffic:	light; moderate to heavy on four-lane stretch

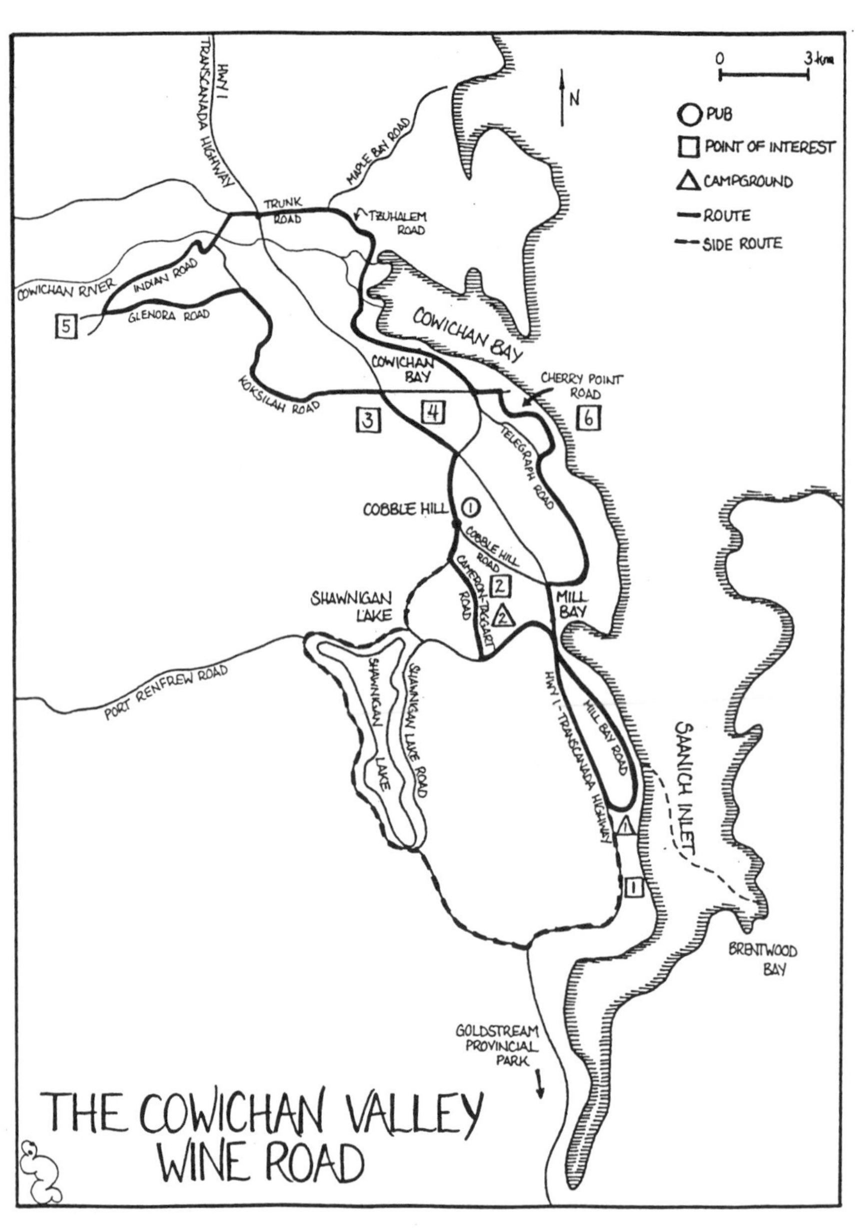

THE COWICHAN VALLEY WINE ROAD
PUB
POINT OF INTEREST
CAMPGROUND
ROUTE
SIDE ROUTE
0
3 km
N
HWY 1 TRANSCANADA HIGHWAY
MAPLE BAY ROAD
TRUNK ROAD
TZUHALEM ROAD
COWICHAN RIVER
INDIAN ROAD
GLENORA ROAD
COWICHAN BAY
KOKSILAH ROAD
CHERRY POINT ROAD
TELEGRAPH ROAD
COBBLE HILL
COBBLE HILL ROAD
CAMERON-TAGGART ROAD
SHAWNIGAN LAKE
MILL BAY
PORT RENFREW ROAD
SHAWNIGAN LAKE ROAD
HWY 1-TRANSCANADA HIGHWAY
MILL BAY ROAD
SAANICH INLET
BRENTWOOD BAY
GOLDSTREAM PROVINCIAL PARK

Services

bank machines:	Mill Bay, Duncan
bike repairs:	Mill Bay, Duncan
liquor store:	Mill Bay, Duncan
groceries:	Mill Bay, Duncan, Cowichan Bay
camping:	Bamberton Provincial Park, few private sites

My approach

The Wine Road can be travelled in one day or two, depending on how long one plans to visit each winery and community. The cyclist's capacity for both consuming wine and hauling bottles back to the campsite will also be a factor. These are good wines, reasonably priced and sufficiently distinct between wineries that you will want to purchase several examples.

The route can be covered in a day by starting and ending at Bamberton Provincial Park. For the two-day trip, consider staying a night at Cherry Point Vineyard. While this is a winery bed and breakfast, BC's only one, the owners also permit occasional camping on the property.

A brief history of Cowichan Valley wineries

Farm wineries are a recent addition to the Island economy, with the first plantings begun in the late 1980s. None has yet reached full production, and all continue to experiment with additional grape varieties suited to the Valley's soils and climate. They are small in scale. To qualify as a farm winery, annual production cannot exceed forty-five thousand litres (ten thousand gallons) of which at least 75 percent must come from from grapes grown on the property. The other 25 percent must originate in BC

Because of this modest scale these wines are available at only a few regular outlets. One is advised to purchase them directly from the winery, or enjoy with a meal at a restaurant featuring any of the Valley's labels. Many of the wines currently produced are white, of German and Italian origin. Each establishment has a tasting room, in which the buyer can sample the winery's offerings and ask questions of the host/proprietor.

The wineries are best visited in the spring and summer when they are fully stocked. As a result of limited production and increasing popularity, later in the year they may be soldout, and therefore closed. I recommend phoning in advance to confirm visiting hours, and have included phone numbers for that purpose.

Bamberton Provincial Park (CG1)

50 sites, swimming, reservations permitted

Bamberton is a large campground and very seldom full. The nearest community is Mill Bay, which can be reached by either the Island Highway, or Mill Bay Road. Both are long downhill routes. This park is an excellent overnight site for cyclists planning to catch the Mill Bay ferry the next day. Just mount up and coast down to the terminal.

The park has a beach which fronts onto the Saanich Inlet, from which on a clear day one can see the snow-capped tip of Mount Baker, a dormant volcano located many kilometres south in Washington State. The park brochure describes the water as "warm." This is a comparative term, and not to be confused with the warm waters of Florida.

Bamberton Site (PI1)

This was once one of the largest cement manufacturing operations on the west coast of North America, and included a company town just above the main industrial site. Cement manufacturing ceased in 1980, having been supplanted by quarries on Texada Island further north, and the site was abandoned. However many of the physical remnants remain.

In the late 1980s a developer who had recognized the site's residential potential proposed building a town there. The resultant demonstrations by environmentalists forced the provincial government to enact a moratorium on development which was still in effect at this writing.

Merridale Cider Works (PI2)

1230 Merridale Road, Cobble Hill (743-4393)

(Cider, Dry Cider, Scrumpy, Cyser)

Merridale Cider is served on tap in many Island pubs. This is an opportunity to visit its place of origin.

If Al Piggott, the owner-operator didn't already exist, he would have to be invented. To meet him is to understand immediately that here is a man who loves his vocation, and sharing it with others. His ciders are made from the 100 percent-undiluted juice of locally grown apples, supplemented by minimal additives to ensure stability. Al will take the time to explain the manufacture of each of his several types of cider, and freely encourages its sampling.

Cider is Alison's beverage of choice so she was keen to absorb any comments that would expand her knowledge of it. Of particular note, Al strongly discourages serving cider with ice, or adding lemon, lime, etc. These are "adulterants" that deteriorate flavour and quality. We also learned that bartenders are not allowed to substitute ice for cider when serving it as draft, unless specifically requested by the customer.

He is prepared to sell his cider by the case to customers, and bus it to them provided they pay the freight. The one-liter bottle fits perfectly in a standard water bottle cage.

Cobblestone Inn (Pub1)

Cobble Hill (743-4232)

This Tudor-style pub was built by Bud Lee in 1983, and he continiues to run it with his daughter. Bud was, and still is, in the restaurant business and it shows. The pub has a diverse menu, food is served in generous portions and is efficiently prepared.The pub derives a large portion of its revenue from the kitchen.

The clientele is an eclectic group comprised of motorists travelling between Victoria and Comox, the loggers and farmers who live and work in the area, white-collar workers who commute to Victoria, and retirees. The casual visitor will immediately be aware of the extraordinarily friendly environment.

This is a great spot to sample the beers from Vancouver Island microbreweries. At this writing the pub had eight such brands on tap.

Bud will accommodate campers in the adjoining vacant field, which may have to be shared with some horses.

Blue Grouse Vineyards (PI3)

4365 Blue Grouse Road, Duncan (743-3834)

(Müller-Thurgau, Ortega, Bacchus, Pinot Gris, Gamay Noir)

Blue Grouse has eighty acres under cultivation, representing a potential annual yield of ten thousand to twenty thousand bottles. The proprietor, Dr. Hans Kiltz, I would describe as politely taciturn. Conversely, Dr. Kiltz would describe me as someone whom he politely wished would go away. He has more productive things to do, like pruning his thousands of vines, which demand a lot of attention year round.

With no prompting he offered that the recent promotion of the Wine Road is in fact a detriment to his business. Currently his entire annual output of predominantly dry German whites is purchased by restaurants and connoisseurs. The casual tourist represents an intrusion on his time and productivity. The operation of a farm winery is labour intensive without the financial margins to hire the extra staff needed to host tasting rooms and answer the sometimes technical questions. He is a perfectionist and the wines he produces reflect this.

Venturi-Schulze Vineyards (PI4)

4235 Trans-Canada Highway, Cobble Hill (743-5630)
(Madeleine Sylvaner; Müller-Thurgau, Pinot Noir, Brut Naturel, Schönburger, Kerner, Millefiori, Pignoletto Aromatico, La Rocca, Balsamic vinegar)

This is the smallest of the Valley wineries and while its product line is currently the most extensive of the Valley wineries, actual output is limited. Marilyn and Giordano Venturi share a passionate commitment to totally natural practices. They add an extra layer of meticulousness to an already demanding profession. Their goal is to make the finest wines in Canada, and "nobody touches our grapes but us."

The entrance to the property is unmarked and visitors are welcome only by prior arrangement, the owners needing to manage their time "to accomplish the control we enjoy over the quality of our product."

Not being a gourmet, it was via Venturi-Schulze that I first became aware of Balsamic vinegar, which is created from wine grapes and is a unique specialty of this vineyard. The tradition of producing Balsamic vinegar began centuries ago in Italy, where it was practiced mostly by families of noble origin who had the necessary vineyards, labour, storage facilities and most importantly, time. Balsamic vinegar is stored in wooden casks for years, sometimes dozens, before it reaches maturity.

Venturi-Schulze Vineyards recently released its first blended vinegar, taken from barrels dated 1970, 1986, 1987 and 1988. A 250 ml bottle sold for $30 with the entire inventory of only 353 bottles being spoken for in advance. The winery hosts winemaker dinners at which the vineyard's wines and vinegar are enjoyed with fine foods. Marilyn Venturi tells me that many cyclists have attended these. Transportation can be arranged.

Vignetti Zanatta (PI5)

5039 Marshall Road, Duncan (748-2338)
(Ortega, Glenora Fantasia Brut, Auxerrois (96))

Vigneti Zanatta is the Island's first farm winery, the family having made wine for its own consumption since the fifties. The premises have a distinct old-world air. The wine tasting room is attached to a traditional farm house and is entered across a terazzo patio, where one is welcome to sit and relax.

Loretta Zanatta is in charge of the wine making. She is a certified enologist, having studied intensively in Italy. Her wines are made in the Italian method, as simply as possible.

Vigneti Zanatta is a place where friends can gather. In fact, volunteers sometimes assist at planting and harvest times, for which they are rewarded with ample Italian-style meals prepared by Loretta's mother. The winery

Cherry Point Vineyards

welcomes tourists. Farm wineries were allowed to sell their wines by the glass for consumption on premise for the first time in 1995, and also to serve food. Loretta looks forward to these changes as an opportunity for the winery to become a gathering place for visiting wine lovers.

Less than a kilometre away is an abandoned railway bed which runs to Lake Cowichan, about 30 km away. Vigneti Zanatta is a perfect location to begin and end that trip, which has also been described in this book.

Cherry Point Vineyards (PI6)

840 Cherry Point Road, Cobble Hill

(Pinot Blanc, Gewürtztraminer, Pinot Noir, Helena, Pinot Auxerrois, Müller-Thurgau)

Cherry Point is the largest of the farm wineries, which is apparent from its large and elaborate buildings and well groomed, expansive grounds. The entrance is marked by a huge wine barrel. It is owned by Helena and Wayne Ulrich, an affable couple commited to extending to visitors the "total experience" of a farm winery. The Ulrich's were among the principals who united the growers and provincial authorities into promoting the Wine Road.

In talking to them we learned of some of the risks of wine growing. A large part of the 1994 crop, an exceptional quality yield, was attacked first by marauding wasps, and then by migrating robins.

As indicated earlier, Cherry Point is also a bed and breakfast, and we learned that Helena's cooking is legendary. They love tourists and frequently host bicycle tours. In fact while not a registered campground, the winery does have a field where occasional campers can pitch tents, and even get access to showers.

The Ulrich's also value marketing and excel at it. They conduct tours of their premises, host special events, for example a wine and food fair, and produce a newsletter.

Side Route — Malahat Drive/Shawnigan Lake

distance:	40 km; circuit
terrain:	extended uphills and downhills, some flat stretches
surface:	two- and four-lane highway with alternating wide and very narrow shoulders; paved two-lane backroads with narrow or no shoulders
traffic:	moderate to heavy on highway; light on backroads

This route is a great workout, pricipally because the Malahat peak is mostly uphill from Bamberton Provincial Park. I recommend travelling this route clockwise from the park. That gets the tough part completed while legs are still fresh. I also suggest an early start, before the considerable vehicle traffic builds.

I have traversed the Malahat on several occasions. Short of taking the Mill Bay ferry to the Saanich Peninsula it is the only way to reach Victoria from up-Island. It is a trip from hell, but worth doing at least once for the challenge. The elevation itself is difficult enough. When combined with extremely narrow shoulders in some places, and speeding cars and trucks, this stretch is downright dangerous. When travelling to Victoria some of the Malahat highway can be by-passed by taking the backroad past Shawnigan Lake, which connects with the highway near the peak.

The views from the two rest areas include the Saanich Peninsula and Gulf Islands. Use extreme caution when entering these. Due to the poor visibility from road level and large volume of traffic, it is prohibited for vehicles to enter if approaching from the north.

The turnoff to Shawnigan Lake is just beyond the rest areas and is a welcome 8- km downhill. From there the route follows either shore of the lake and returns to the highway.

Cowichan Lake

Our Logging Past

Cowichan Lake refers to the lake and surrounding area; Lake Cowichan is the village at the east end of the lake. The area is reached on Highway 4 from Duncan, an easy 30-km cycle on wide, paved shoulders over long, rolling hills.

I had visited Cowichan Lake many times before realizing the extent to which it exemplified the early years of the Island's modern economy. From the 1880s to the 1950s the lake was a bustling logging centre employing hundreds. Logs harvested from the surrounding forests were dumped into the lake where they were towed to local mills or loaded on trains and hauled to the coast. There were three railway lines into the area and countless spurs.

The forestry industry still provides 70 percent of the area's employment, but that now represents far fewer jobs, many at the Youbou mill and vulnerable to periodic shut-downs. There is still evidence of the area's previous economic prominence in the form of company houses, old railway beds, log sorts, and various dilapidated structures.

Attempts to kick-start tourism have met with some success, but Lake Cowichan is still a little too far off the beaten path for many Island visitors. Because I grew up in populous eastern Ontario, where small out-of the-way places like Lake Cowichan are tourist mecca's, I keep waiting for its tourism base to explode. It's a wonderful spot for the family that enjoys being outdoors.

I have departed from the main route/side route format for this chapter in favour of describing three distinct routes. Each is a circuit, and each has Gordon Bay Provincial Park as its hub. One circuit is deserted railway bed, the other two are mostly logging roads. The only paved sections are

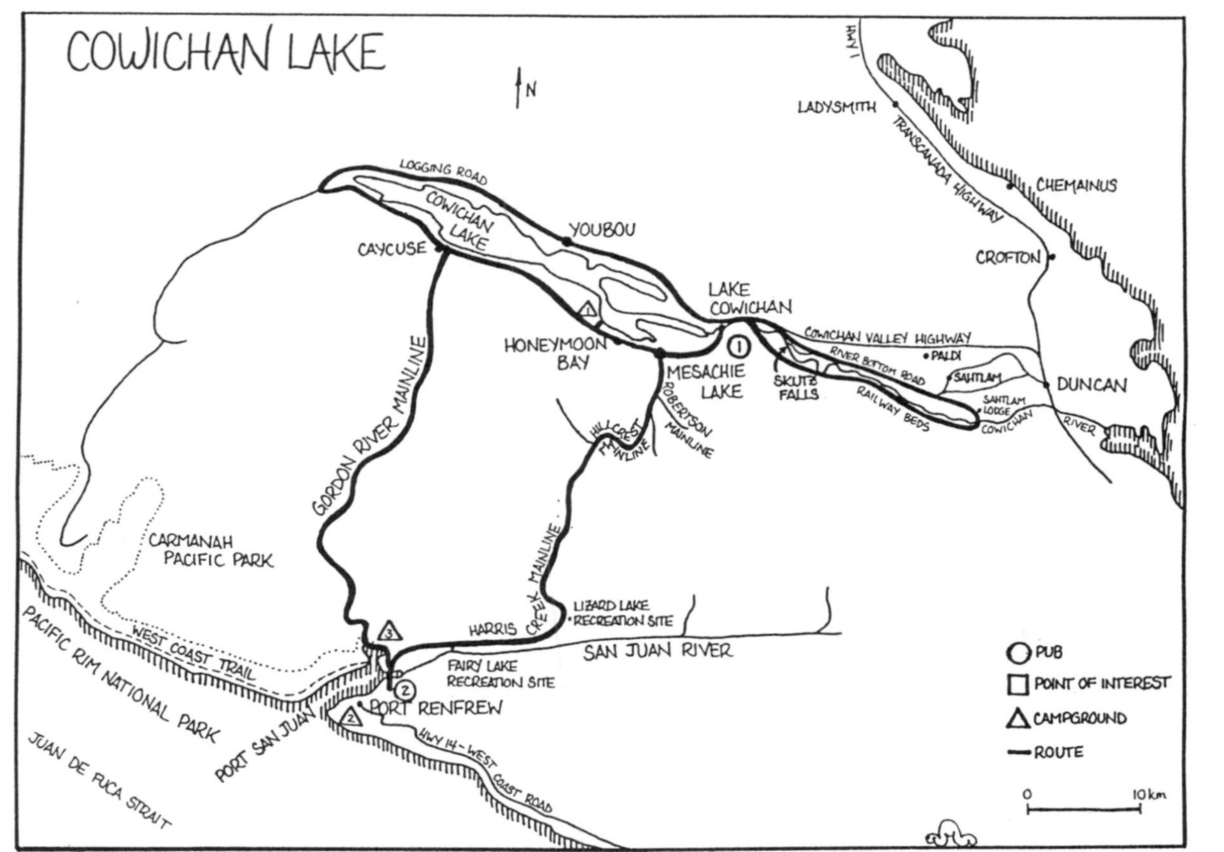
COWICHAN LAKE
N
HWY 1
LADYSMITH
TRANSCANADA HIGHWAY
CHEMAINUS
CROFTON
LOGGING ROAD
COWICHAN LAKE
YOUBOU
CAYCUSE
LAKE COWICHAN
COWICHAN VALLEY HIGHWAY
PALDI
RIVER BOTTOM ROAD
SAHTLAM
DUNCAN
SAHTLAM LODGE
COWICHAN
RIVER
RAILWAY BEDS
SKUTZ FALLS
HONEYMOON BAY
MESACHIE LAKE
ROBERTSON MAINLINE
HILLCREST MAINLINE
GORDON RIVER MAINLINE
HARRIS CREEK MAINLINE
LIZARD LAKE RECREATION SITE
SAN JUAN RIVER
FAIRY LAKE RECREATION SITE
CARMANAH PACIFIC PARK
WEST COAST TRAIL
PACIFIC RIM NATIONAL PARK
PORT RENFREW
PORT SAN JUAN
HWY 14 - WEST COAST ROAD
JUAN DE FUCA STRAIT
PUB
POINT OF INTEREST
CAMPGROUND
ROUTE
0
10 km

some stretches at the east end of Cowichan Lake, and approaching and leaving Port Renfrew.

The forestry information centre, located in a conspicuous log building at the west end of the village of Lake Cowichan, distributes free maps of area logging roads. I recommend obtaining one, particularly for the ride to Port Renfrew.

Services

bank machines:	Lake Cowichan
bike repairs:	Lake Cowichan (limited), Duncan
liquor stores:	Lake Cowichan, Port Renfrew (general store)
groceries:	Lake Cowichan, Youbou, Port Renfrew
camping:	Gordon Bay Provincial Park, numerous private and primitive sites
hospital:	Duncan

Gordon Bay Provincial Park (CG1)

131 sites, washrooms, showers, swimming, reservations permitted

Located in a second-growth Douglas fir forest, this is a large campground. Accessible to the lake, it is reportedly one of the first areas logged on the Island. Notched stumps of the original forest are still evident. Fallers wedged springboards into them to facilitate working above the dense underbrush.

The sites are well-spaced and private. The park has a large beach, and in the summer the water temperature is comfortable. Campers who are empty-nesters, or don't appreciate children, beware. This park has lots of them, a consequence of the beach.

My approach

I recommend spending several days in this area, and using Gordon Bay Provincial Park as a home base from which to explore the individual routes. While each can be covered in a day, the trip to Port Renfrew is the most physically demanding. Since this village is also worth taking some time to visit, the cyclist may want to consider overnighting there.

The trips in this area are almost entirely off-road. I recommend wide tires, and carrying a spare tire and inner tube. This is also a good time to start thinking about using that portable water purifier. Logging roads can be dusty and hot, and while water is available, it's all from streams and potentially harmful.

It is tempting, particularly after perusing a map of the logging roads, to consider cycling to Carmannah Pacific Park from Lake Cowichan. Carmannah is a valley of old-growth forest with some of the world's oldest and tallest trees. Sitka spruce some twenty storeys high. Recently the valley was saved from harvesting and added to Pacific Rim National Park. I recommend visiting, it is a truly mystical experience, but not by bike. The roads are pretty rough, sometimes busy with tourists, and the area is still actively logged.

A brief history of logging on the Island

I am indebted to Robert D. Turner who in his wonderful book, *Logging by Rail, The British Columbia Story*, provided much of the background information for this chapter.

When I was growing up in Kingston, Ontario, there were two subjects in polite conversation that one routinely avoided, politics and religion. So much of the community's sentiments polarized around these two topics that were broached only if the Canadiens and Maple Leafs hadn't played each other recently, and a person badly needed to stir the pot. On the Island we have no such sports rivalries, but opinions on logging can reduce all other social issues to insignificant sidebars.

For all its controversy, logging for profit on the west coast has a history of only one hundred years. That was when it became mechanized. Before then the forest was never really perceived as an asset. It hindered farming, settlement and mining, the serious money makers of the time. Any trees that were harvested were used for local buildings and structures, after being transformed into lumber by small nearby mills.

Douglas fir was the most commercially valued. It was strong, durable and adaptable to most structural applications. And accessible; a key consideration given the technology of the day. Other species also gained favour as expanding settlement in North America and abroad increased demand for west coast wood. This in turn led to more mills, which needed a reliable and steady supply of wood. Increased mechanization in the harvesting and transportation of trees would ensure this.

A century ago the commercially accessible supply of old-growth forest must have seemed inexhaustible. Much of this has now vanished, replaced by second- and third-growth plantings. Little or no value was placed on the aesthetic and recreational value of forests, and general concern for the old-growth forest as a delicate ecosystem and "as vital reserves for biological and cultural diversity" (Robert D. Turner) is relatively recent.

Confrontations between those wanting to harvest old-growth forest for profit or their livelihoods, and those wishing to preserve them, occur often on the Island. They attract worldwide media attention. The issues are complex, bitter, occasionally violent and far from resolved.

Route — The Cowichan River Railway Beds

distance:	42 km; circuit
terrain:	extended flat stretches
surface:	abandoned railway bed, trestles; paved two-lane near Lake Cowichan
traffic:	very light; occasional dirt bike and 4X4

Like most small boys, I'm fascinated by trains. I still own an electric train set, and while I haven't played with it for years, I would never consider selling it. So when first informed of the railway beds on each side of the Cowichan River, it was only natural that I explore them, and research their history.

I recommend beginning this route on the old Esquimalt & Nanaimo bed which runs along the north side of the valley and can be accessed at the east end of the village of Lake Cowichan, across the road from the Infocentre. The access is unmarked and the bed obscured by a line of trees, but trust me, it's there. Once on the bed, follow your nose. The route follows behind houses, across roads and along the edge of the valley. A few stretches are thick with broom, but all are passable. The E&N transported logs down the valley to the large mills and log dumps at Crofton, Chemainus and Ladysmith and mills along the line. "A 1944 article noted that more than thirty-seven thousand cars of logs had been hauled in the previous three years" (Robert D. Turner).

Leave the bed at Cowichan Lake Road, about 14 km from the start and follow the signs to the Sahtlam Lodge, a distance of about 4 km. A brief ride in a hand-propelled cable car owned by the lodge lands the rider on the other side of the Cowichan River at the base of the old CNR bed. A 7.5-km ride downriver takes the cyclist to Glenora, on the outskirts of Duncan.

Upriver is the return trip to Lake Cowichan. The CNR hauled logs to Cowichan Bay at the mouth of the river, and to Victoria. This stretch includes several trestles with closed signs that people just ignore. Some of the trestles are engineering marvels, but missing a few cross ties, and therefore unnerving in spots. In a couple of places near Skutz Falls the bed is overgrown or ditched and it is necessary to detour briefly. Skutz Falls is the site of a picturesque riverside campground, which is popular with young people in the summer, and a fish ladder. The outskirts of Lake Cowichan are another 5 km or so up the line. Any road to the right will lead to downtown.

Railway logging on the Island

The adaptation of railway logging to Vancouver Island was driven by one factor, the need to keep the mills supplied with logs. Conventional methods of the time employed livestock and steam "donkeys" to haul logs. But these had exhausted all the available forest. Trains were needed to expand the mills' raw-material base.

The Island's first logging railroad began supplying the Chemainus mill in 1900. By the end of the twenties, the boom years of coastal logging railways, there were twelve logging railroads operating on Vancouver Island. Trackage hit a peak of about 1200 km. Railway logging had levelled by the forties, and declined very rapidly thereafter. By the fifties, when the railways of North America were converting to diesel, the logging companies were converting to trucks. The old-growth forest that had been accessible by train was gone. And trucks and road-building technique had reached a point that allowed previously inaccessible forests to be harvested more efficiently by truck. Railway logging is now practiced only on the north Island.

Aside from a few locomotives preserved as exhibits, the only evidence of this short but hectic period in the Island's history are the railbeds. Those in the Cowichan Valley are the best I have found. They may not have been built to trans-continental standards because it was unnecessary — they were a specialized application with a finite life span. Nevertheless they have endured remarkably well. Some of the fills, cuts and in particular the trestles, are remarkable accomplishments for the technology of the time. They are also a testimonial to the wealth that could be derived from logging.

To learn more about this period in Island history visit the museums in Lake Cowichan and Duncan. The latter has an operating train.

Rail's End Pub (Pub1)

Across the park from the museum (749-6755)

Built in 1992 on the former site of the village railway yard, the pub's architecture resembles a railway station. The owner, Ron Girrard has a passion for model trains, and his pub is adorned with his collection of engines and rolling stock, some manufactured in the twenties and thirties.

Ron also shared with me that the basement of the pub is the home of the Lake Cowichan Model Railway Club. An ongoing project is a scale recreation of the village as it existed in the thirties and forties. At this writing members had hand-laid an estimated 30,000 miniature ties.

Dave Moddle at Cowichan Lake

Route — Port Renfrew via the Logging Roads

distance:	108 km; circuit
terrain:	extended hills, one steep; extended flat stretches
surface:	two-lane or less, loose gravel, dusty; paved two-lane entering and leaving Port Renfrew
traffic:	light, mostly logging trucks and pick-ups

This route is well marked. It begins at the entrance to the Gordon River mainline, a logging road whose entrance can be found just west of the turnoff into the provincial park. The road follows Sutton Creek steadily uphill for 8 km, and crosses a peak to begin a steady 30 km descent, with a few intervening hills, along the Gordon River into Port Renfrew. The return trip along the Harris Creek mainline is mostly flat and paved for the first 18 km. Where the pavement ends there begins a steady and sometimes steep ascent, before connecting with the Hillcrest mainline and beginning a steady descent back to Cowichan Lake.

The road surface, particularly on the return route, is mostly gravel but well maintained to accommodate the logging trucks and private vehicles that use it as the main thoroughfare to the Cowichan Valley. This is cougar, bear and elk country, with sightings of the last two species common. The scenery is mountainous and rugged, with some of the vistas having been enhanced by clear-cut logging. Clear-cuts are not pretty sights. Operators in the San Juan Valley have been publicly censured for destroying the landscape and salmon spawning habitat as a result of past indiscriminate practices.

If staying at Port Renfrew overnight, consider either Port Renfrew Marina and Campground, or Trailhead Campsite. Camping is also permitted on the Reserve's beach, a location with a spectacular view across the harbour, but I am told security there is inadequate. There are a couple of primitive lakeshore campgrounds, at Fairy Lake and Lizard Lake, near the beginning of the return route on the Harris Creek mainline.

Port Renfrew

This village of 350 represents another milestone in my writing career. It was the subject of my first article to be rejected. On our initial trip there via the logging roads Alison and I discovered that the only bridge into town had been washed out by logs during the winter rains, some say a consequence of years of careless clear-cutting. The bridge also separated the Indian Reserve from the white community. Flushed with success at having recently sold my first article, this represented a chance to write an essay that would change the world. A cultural chasm in Canadian society symbolized by a washed out bridge. If the reader has perceived no improvements in cultural interaction in Canada, that is because my completed article was not worth publishing.

However, because I had returned several times for research, I learned much about Port Renfrew. It began as farm homesteads in the 1880s, but by the early 1900s was a major logging centre. The old-growth timber was accessible and easily boomed thanks to a large natural harbour. During the forties and fifties several logging companies employed hundreds of men here, harvesting assisted by a network of rail and truck roads, the remnants of which are still evident. Like other Vancouver Island logging communities, Port Renfrew experienced rapid economic decline in the seventies and eighties. The post office manager, a fourth-generation resident, remembers when two hundred families made their living from the woods. Now there are twelve. I can recall speculation several years ago that Port Renfrew could become a ghost town.

Attractions include kilometres of hiking and off-road cycling trails, Botanical Beach Provincial Park (no bikes allowed) an intertidal research centre, and the southern terminus of the West Coast Trail. This connects Port Renfrew in the south to Bamfield, 80 km to the north. It was originally created in the days of sail to enable shipwrecked sailors to return to civilization from what was then known as "the Graveyard of the Pacific." It is now attracts hikers from all over the world.

Trailhead Campsite (CG2)

10 sites, enclosed cooking shelter with wood stove, reasonable rates, showers and laundry nearby.

This small campground is located just above the hotel at the government wharf, and is owned by the operator of the ferry to the West Coast Trail. It is a cozy, quiet spot and just a short walk downhill to the hotel pub, the only watering hole in town.

A welcome feature is the cooking shelter, enclosed on three sides and heated by a wood stove and plenty of nearby fuel; it's a convenient place to dry out wet gear.

There are showers and a laundromat in the out-building just across from the hotel.

Port Renfrew Marina and Campground (CG3)

100 sites, some riverside

This is a textbook example of turning an economic "sow's ear into a silk purse." When logging was king this was a log sort, where timber was collected and boomed in the nearby river. The heritage of the departing logging company was several hectares of asphalt and a series of pylons protruding from the river. The present owner leased the property a few years ago and converted it to an RV campsite and marina. In the summer hundreds of families arrive towing their boats and eager to fish for salmon. The location doesn't yet compete aesthetically with a provincial park, but every year there are a few more improvements.

The owner will also provide information on the network of local logging roads, ideal for mountain biking, and the route to the top of Brown Mountain. From here, at an elevation of 600 m one can oversee San Juan Bay, the Strait and the Olympic Peninsula on the American side.

Port Renfrew Hotel (Pub2)

Top of the government wharf (647-5541)

Every small community has a place where the local citizenry gather to bond, usually under the guise of solving the world's problems. In Port Renfrew this is the hotel pub. It is a venue in which the casual visitor who opts to remain unobtrusive can learn much about this unique little town.

Route — Around the Lake

distance:	76 km; circuit
terrain:	short rolling hills, one long steep hill, long flat stretches
surface:	two-lane or less, loose gravel, dusty; paved two-lane at east end of lake, both sides
traffic:	light

This route circumvents Cowichan Lake, the largest freshwater body on the Island. It's a good workout with the opportunity to pass through the remnants of the camps and settlements from the boom years. The view from the top of the hill just past the turn off to the Gordon River mainline includes much of the lake. We usually start at the Riverside Inn in Lake Cowichan, and travel clockwise. That way the long stretch of paved road after Youbou is at the end of the route, and lessens some of the fatigue.

Because it is loose gravel this road can get very dusty in the summer. Dust from passing vehicles hangs in the air, impeding breathing and obscuring vision. Alternatively, if the road is wet, count on getting covered with mud unless you have fenders.

The Riverside Inn has a raft tied to the river bank just down from the parking lot. A dive from this removes dust and sweat before entering the Inn for a cold one.

North Cowichan

"No machine can replace me
until it learns to drink."
(a sign in the Crofton Hotel)

I cycle this region often. We find it a pleasant change of venue to transport our bikes here by car from home in Nanaimo, and then spend a day touring the route, or part of it. In addition, for the past four years my daughter has been attending university in Victoria, and I ride through North Cowichan in order to retrieve my car from her — an act sometimes needed to re-affirm my ownership of this vehicle.

Although North Cowichan tries to define itself as a tourist destination, the most notable features of its landscape are its farms and mills. The farms produce vegetables, poultry and dairy products for Victoria, Nanaimo and Vancouver. The mills are mainly situated on the waterfront between Crofton and Ladysmith. Now consolidated to a few large-scale operations, they are the descendants of many more operations that were strung along this coast earlier in the century. Here they could take advantage of accessible raw material, the railway, and sheltered harbours for processing and shipping logs.

The route, except for the Island Highway, is a reasonably traffic-free trip through modern Island history and provides great exercise with the potential for plenty of pub-hopping. The roads are a combination of backroads and the Island Highway. The backroads are typical Vancouver Island — two-lane paved, narrow or no shoulders, winding and hilly and a few extended flat stretches. Traffic is usually light. The Island Highway between Duncan and Ladysmith is all four-lane, with wide shoulders and mostly long but gradual hills. Traffic is moderate, sometimes heavy, and always fast.

While each town on the route has more than one pub except Genoa

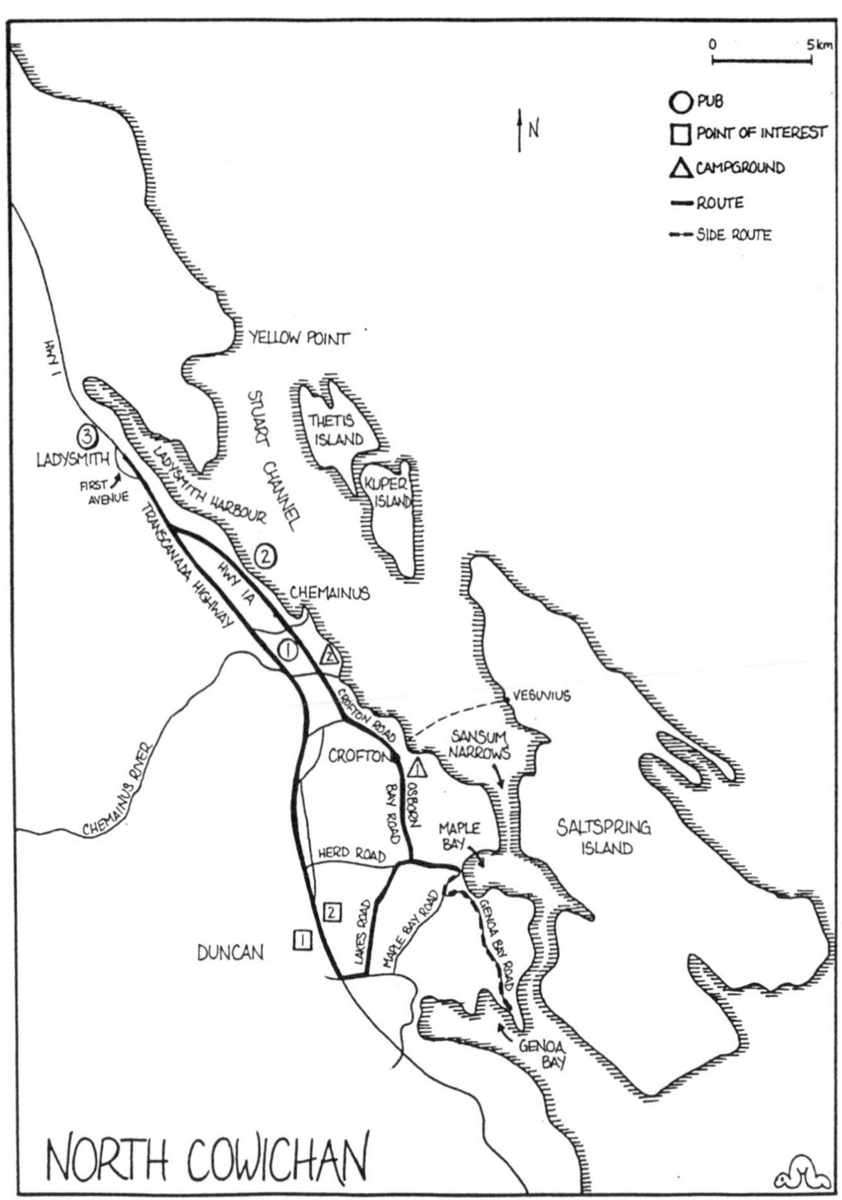
0
5km
PUB
POINT OF INTEREST
CAMPGROUND
ROUTE
SIDE ROUTE
N
YELLOW POINT
HWY 1
STUART CHANNEL
THETIS ISLAND
KUPER ISLAND
LADYSMITH
FIRST AVENUE
LADYSMITH HARBOUR
TRANSCANADA HIGHWAY
HWY 1A
CHEMAINUS
CROFTON ROAD
VESUVIUS
SANSUM NARROWS
CHEMAINUS RIVER
CROFTON
OSBORN BAY ROAD
MAPLE BAY
SALTSPRING ISLAND
HERD ROAD
LAKES ROAD
MAPLE BAY ROAD
GENOA BAY ROAD
DUNCAN
GENOA BAY
NORTH COWICHAN

Bay (which has none), there are only a few private campgrounds and no provincial parks.

Main Route

Road

distance:	63 km; circuit
terrain:	hills, some steep; several extended flat stretches
surface:	paved two-lane backroads, narrow or no shoulders; four-lane highway, wide shoulders
traffic:	light on backroads; moderate to heavy on highway

Services

bank machines:	Duncan, Chemainus, Ladysmith
bike repairs:	Duncan, Ladysmith
liquor store:	Duncan, Chemainus, Ladysmith
groceries:	Duncan, Crofton, Chemainus, Ladysmith
camping:	a few private campgrounds (none in Maple Bay or Genoa Bay)
hospital:	Duncan, Chemainus, Ladysmith

My approach

I ride this route for two purposes. One is as a thoroughfare to Duncan or Crofton, on my way to the south Island or Salt Spring respectively. If in a hurry, the Island Highway is by far the fastest way to accomplish this. However it has more traffic, and lacks the scenery and watering holes of the backroads.

We tour the circular route for exercise and fun. Although any of the communities on the map represent practical starting points, if camping I recommend Crofton or Chemainus, with their nearby campgrounds. Also, as the map indicates, this region can be divided into shorter individual routes while still remaining circuits.

A modern history of the region

Today this area possesses an almost pastoral air. Small communities nestle among farms and fields, connected by winding two-lane backroads. The region's lumber and pulp mills, originally its raison d'être and still operating, resemble quietly vaporous industrial afterthoughts in an otherwise peaceful rural setting.

A quick reference to North Cowichan's history reveals that it was anything but quiet. From the late 1800s until after WWII it was hyperactive with logging, milling and sometimes mining. The noise from the trains, trucks, mills and smelters must have been incessant. While the region's mining history was brief, the forest industry continues, but radically changed. New technology, environmental and land-use strategies, and international competition have created a leaner, cleaner and more efficient industry.

When I began researching this chapter I expected to find a forest harvesting and manufacturing sector in decline and being replaced by tourism and retirement. The latter are definitely significant factors. But rather than replace, they augment a robust forest sector that is still the region's largest employer. It quietly goes about its business of producing some of the world's finest lumber and pulp products, much for export to Europe, the USA and Asia.

All the communities in the region have strong ties to the forest sector and consequently have experienced much recent change. The early '80s were tough times for forest companies. A growing awareness of raw material shortages, environmental concerns, competition, escalating labour costs and depressed prices induced by recession exposed the inefficiencies of Island mills. Owners responded by modernizing or shutting down or both, resulting in massive permanent and temporary job losses. The Island became economically depressed. House prices fell to less than half their pre-recession highs.

This period also contributed to our recovery. In the mid and late eighties Canadians from other provinces, particularly eastern Ontario whose mainly industrial economy had super-heated, began to migrate here in droves. They were lured by our lifestyle, competitive house prices, and the appeal of realizing the equity in their homes whose prices had sky-rocketed beyond their wildest dreams. Between 1986 and 1991 the population of the Cowichan Region alone increased by 15 percent. These "urban refugees" brought with them the skills and buying power to expand the Island's economy.

North Cowichan, always productive agriculturally, also began to develop its light manufacturing and tourism sectors. The forest sector has since recovered, resulting in a robust but more diverse regional economy.

Duncan

The commercial centre for the Cowichan Valley, Duncan began life as a railway station on the recently completed E&N. Newcomers could arrive by rail and settle, then transport their produce to market on it. At the turn of the century Duncan was briefly a distribution centre for mining activities in the surrounding hills. This was short-lived but replaced by sawmills and farming. In the early 1900s so many of the new settlers to the area produced poultry that it was known as the "Egg Basket of the World." Today, with a population of just under 5,000, Duncan serves over 66,000 people in the area.

Downtown Duncan is decorated by forty-one totem poles. To the aboriginal peoples of the Pacific Northwest totem poles are a substitute for written history. They are an archive of myths, legends, genealogy and other important events. This downtown area, flat and central, is one of the most convenient on the Island to tour by cycle.

Native Heritage Centre (PI1)

With approximately 3,000 members, the Cowichan Indian Band is the largest band in BC. The reserve adjoins the south end of Duncan and includes part of Duncan's commercial area, which is leased from the band.

The Heritage Centre, a complex owned and operated by the band, is a showcase for Coast Salish culture and art, and a teaching centre dedicated to the education of band members.

BC Forestry Museum (PI2)

This museum documents and preserves a century of Vancouver Island logging history. Located on a hundred acres it includes indoor and outdoor displays, and an old-growth forest. The outdoor exhibits include equipment and old-style living quarters. An operational steam-driven passenger train takes visitors on a twenty-minute ride through the grounds.

Forestry formed much of Vancouver Island. I am grateful to the museum for allowing me access to its library for my research.

Maple Bay

This village of marinas is a popular place for boaters from as far away as Duncan, Victoria and Nanaimo to moor their craft. It provides quick access to the Gulf Islands. For anyone interested in viewing a fascinating alternative lifestyle, Maple Bay also harbours a large selection of houseboats.

The village has a pub at each end. We favour the Brigantine Inn at the north end because it is open more regularly than its counterpart to the south. This pub overlooks the government wharf, a small floating dock that I can never view without recalling one of my spectacular boating faux pas. We were spending our vacation sailing in the Gulf Islands and decided to put in at Maple Bay. Because the wind was blowing from a favourable direction I planned to sail right up to my mooring. Our normal practice had been to lower sails and motor in, so this was my first attempt at this manoeuvre. The two fellows intently fishing on the dock would not witness this act of nautical competence because they were facing away from us.

Had the main sheet not fouled, thereby preventing me from luffing the main sail and slowing the boat, I would have succeeded. A 13,000-pound vessel under sail makes absolutely no noise until it hits the dock. The ensuing snapping and crunching was augmented by the sputtering and cussing of the unsuspecting fisherman I had just knocked into the bay. Fortunately, aside from a scratch on the hull my boat was undamaged.

Maple Bay has no campground.

Genoa Bay

Genoa Bay is a hilly 7-km (one way) side trip from Maple Bay. Until 1928 it was the site of one of the largest saw mills in the province. It is now comprised of a marina, a restaurant and a few residences.

The village has neither pub nor campground.

Crofton

Crofton, population 1,800, began as a copper smelter in 1902. Ore was hauled on a narrow-gauge railway from a mine in Mount Sicker several kilometres inland. After a series of financial failures and near failures it closed permanently in 1908. All that remains today of its complex of rail sidings, piers and buildings are some tailings on the beach and a few pilings in the bay. A detailed model of the operation sits in the museum near the ferry dock.

The pulp and paper mill 1 km to the north opened in 1958 and employs fifteen hundred, many of whom commute to work from other parts of the region. It manufactures newsprint, paper and pulp for export around the world and has invested millions in environmental protection measures. The mill is open for tours on weekdays during the summer.

Crofton has two pubs. The Crofton Hotel, close to the campsite and ferry dock, is a working man's beer parlor — often noisy, always smoky and great for people-watching. This bar is the only place in town to withdraw cash by bank card.

The Brass Bell Pub, near the top of the hill from the ferry, is a more traditional neighbourhood pub and a convenient spot to await the ferry from Vesuvius.

Osborne Bay Resort (CG1)

42 sites, washrooms, showers, swimming

This new private campground, composed of neatly tiered waterfront sites facing Salt Spring Island, is on the site of the old copper smelter. When it was originally purchased by its current owners, a family which had recently emigrated from England, it was covered with slag. They trucked this away, landscaped the property, and installed the sites and structures. To quote the owner, "What may be worthless to the locals is viewed differently by an outsider."

The resort is a convenient location to start and end this route, or catch the ferry to Salt Spring.

Bald Eagle Campsite (CG2)

30 sites, washrooms, showers

This private facility offers quiet, rustic sites in a wooded area on the edge of the Chemainus River. Chemainus, the nearest community, is a mostly level ride 5 km to the north.

I first stopped here by myself one fall evening. After supper I realized there was considerable animal noise from the river on the other side of the trees from my campsite. On investigation I encountered hundreds of spawning salmon. The noise was critters feeding on and arguing over their bodies.

Chemainus

One of the oldest European settlements on Vancouver Island, farming here began in the 1850s. However, by the 1860s Chemainus had evolved into a one-industry lumber town. The last of its sawmills, also one of the world's largest, shut down in 1983, eliminating the town's entire industrial labour force. It subsequently reopened as one of the world's most technologically advanced. But modernization and downsizing had reduced staff to one hundred from the previous five hundred.

Chemainus, population 3,900, was confronted with having to recreate itself or become a ghost town. With the guidance of business and civic leaders it became "the little town that did" by transforming itself into Canada's largest permanent outdoor art gallery. Artists have painted thirty-two murals depicting the town's history on the walls of downtown buildings. The town attracts over three hundred thousand visitors a year.

Not being a town of diminutives, it has also begun creating the Artisan Village, which when completed will attract and house artists and artisans from all around the Pacific Rim.

If planning to spend more than a day in the area, I recommend the thirty-five minute ferry ride from Chemainus to Thetis Island. Thetis has about 20 km of paved and hilly roads that represent a good workout, and a pub in the "gap" that separates it from Kuper Island. Don't be surprised if you smell coffee as the ferry pulls into Preedy Harbour. There is a coffee roasting company up the road that produces custom blends for subscribers around the world. The ferry also stops at Kuper. This is a First Nations Reserve and non-aboriginals are unwelcome.

Horseshoe Bay Inn (Pub1)

9576 Chemainus Road (246-4535)

Horseshoe Bay was Chemainus' original name. The Inn is a heritage hotel, having been established in 1892. It is a congenial spot, and although it features "real food for a realistic price," we seldom eat there. We arrive too early to be hungry.

The entrance is on the main street. I recommend locking bikes together before entering. Alternatively, when I travel alone the management has never objected to my bike accompanying me inside.

Saltair Pub (Pub2)

midway between Chemainus and Ladysmith (246-4942)

This comfortable old former country home, complete with stone fireplace and wing-backed chairs, is set in the trees amid an expanse of lawns. When cycling home from the south I always drop in. Its affable owner, Vern Byers always makes a point of greeting us, and his kitchen serves the best burgers on the Island. Vern permits camping in a private, lawned area behind his pub.

When I last chatted with Vern he was investigating implemeting two- and three-day guided cycling tours of the area. These would include being met at the Nanaimo ferry terminal, camping, showers, meals and pub stops.

Ladysmith

First known as Oyster Bay, Ladysmith was named after a victorious battle in the Boer War which took place at Ladysmith, South Africa. It was founded by coal baron Robert Dunsmuir to provide living space for miners and their families who worked at the Extension coal mines 18 km to the north. Many buildings, some of which still stand, were moved to this site via rail and oxen.

In 1904 Ladysmith boasted a population of five thousand and a booming economy. In 1931 the coal ran out, but five years later the town re-emerged as a logging community, courtesy of several thousand old-growth trees that had blown down behind town in a 1931 gale. During this period Ladysmith developed an extensive railyard to serve the logging industry. The remnants of this, including deserted buildings and decaying rolling stock remain at the bottom of town, easily visible from the highway.

Main street, a few blocks uphill from the highway, features vintage buildings, many of which have been refurbished to their original conditions. There is a remarkable concentration of hotel pubs here. Included among these are three hotel pubs situated less than a block apart, a heritage of the "boom town" days when Ladysmith contained over twenty such establishments.

With a current population of less than five thousand, in the early eighties this town looked to be down for the count. But civic pride, downtown revitalization, and affordable housing have restored its growth.

Ladysmith Inn (Pub3)

640 First Avenue (245-8033)

Opened in 1911, this was a popular drinking place for the local miners. It has just been completely and expensively refurbished in wood and brass to recreate the decor of its era. At one end of the floor is a huge antique pool table. Anxious to preserve its condition, management insists on receiving security from would-be players. The owners do not welcome bicycles on the premises, but will provide a secure spot in the back doorway.

Nanaimo

My Home Town

When I first conceived this book, I expected this to be the most challenging chapter to write. I didn't disappoint myself. In the other route descriptions I have attempted to impart to the reader, likely to be a first-time visitor, my observations and experiences as a frequent visitor. My format for those chapters doesn't quite apply here. I'm more than a frequent visitor; I live here.

More importantly, my knowledge and experience of Nanaimo is intensely personal. This makes it difficult for me to distinguish between locations that I value, and those likely to be of most interest to the reader and cycling camper. I love this city. Having lived and worked in large cities most of my adult life and hated it, Nanaimo has given me an opportunity for personal renewal. It is a friendly, energetic community with most of the work and lifestyle options of a big city without being one. Moreover the terrain here is ideal for cycling. The rider can choose between flat and hilly, in surroundings that are urban, rural or wilderness. My nine years here have reaffirmed my passion for cycling and the outdoors, and in the process I have acquired some of my closest friends and associates.

To me, Nanaimo's main flaw is in not always being bicycle friendly. The city has grown rapidly, and its streets are often more crowded than they were designed to be. Its drivers, many of whom are visitors and tourists, are not yet accustomed to the growing number of cyclists on the roads. In addition the volume of traffic on the Island Highway which runs through the centre of the city, increases substantially with the arrival and departure of ferries to the mainland. In summer this occurs hourly. Also to be noted, the Island Highway has no shoulders from where it enters the city from the south until well north of the downtown area. Cyclists

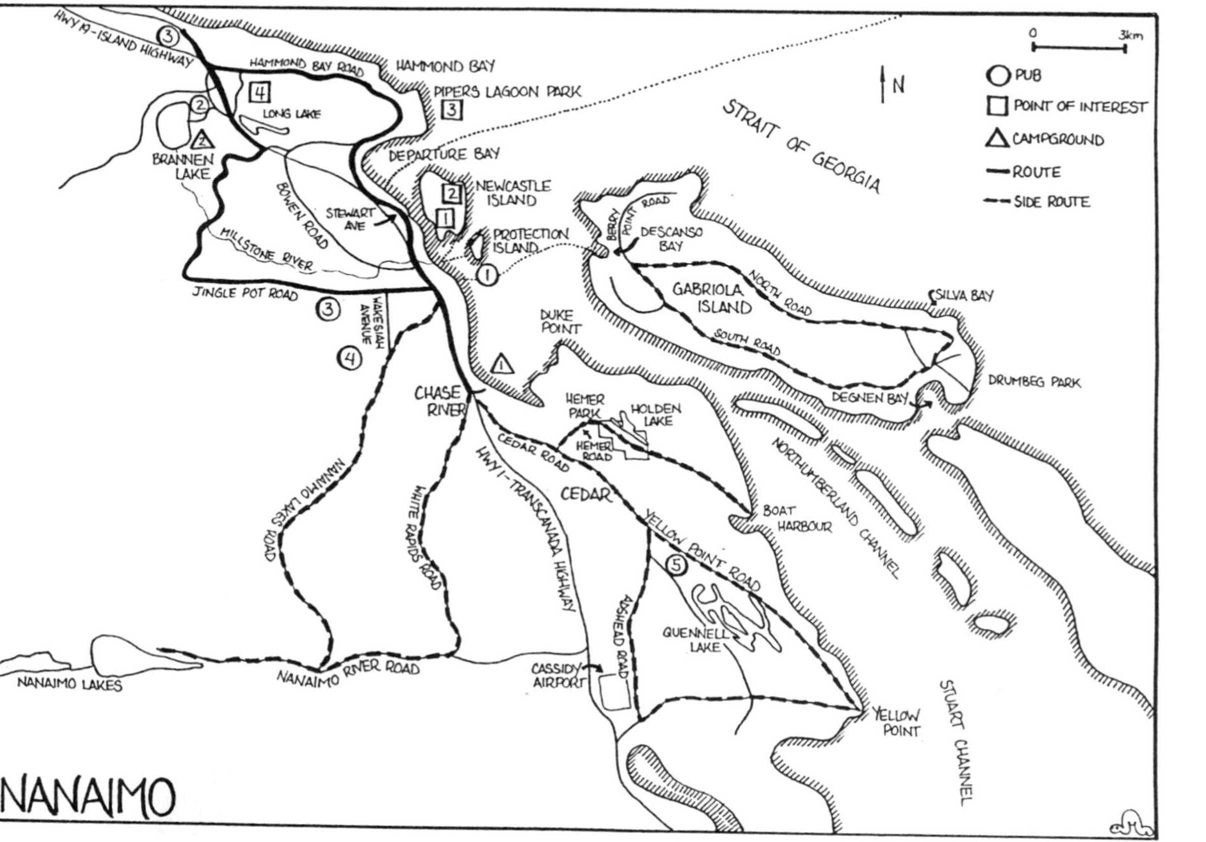
NANAIMO
0
3km
N
PUB
POINT OF INTEREST
CAMPGROUND
ROUTE
SIDE ROUTE
HWY 19-ISLAND HIGHWAY
HAMMOND BAY ROAD
HAMMOND BAY
PIPERS LAGOON PARK
LONG LAKE
BRANNEN LAKE
DEPARTURE BAY
NEWCASTLE ISLAND
PROTECTION ISLAND
STRAIT OF GEORGIA
BOWEN ROAD
STEWART AVE
MILLSTONE RIVER
JINGLE POT ROAD
WAKESIAH AVENUE
BERRY POINT ROAD
DESCANSO BAY
GABRIOLA ISLAND
NORTH ROAD
SOUTH ROAD
SILVA BAY
DUKE POINT
DRUMBEG PARK
DEGNEN BAY
CHASE RIVER
HEMER PARK
HOLDEN LAKE
HEMER ROAD
CEDAR ROAD
CEDAR
NANAIMO LAKES ROAD
WHITE RAPIDS ROAD
HWY 1-TRANSCANADA HIGHWAY
NORTHUMBERLAND CHANNEL
BOAT HARBOUR
YELLOW POINT ROAD
ADSHEAD ROAD
QUENNELL LAKE
CASSIDY AIRPORT
NANAIMO RIVER ROAD
NANAIMO LAKES
YELLOW POINT
STUART CHANNEL

should avoid this by taking side streets. Since we have lived here there has been at least one cycling fatality on this stretch.

By the time this book reaches the stores there will be a second highway. A four-lane, limited-access by-pass being constructed to the west of the city will augment the existing road through Nanaimo. Not only is this expected to decrease traffic volume on the old highway, it will also have its own parallel cycle trail.

In this chapter I assume the role of tour guide. The reader is a newcomer to the city, and plans to stay for a few days. I have volunteered to lead a series of cycling tours and provide appropriate commentary, a notion which will have many of my friends in stitches, familiar as they are with my less than gregarious nature. The main route includes Nanaimo's harbour area, central to its existence since its beginning, and extends to the north end, the focus of its growth and now more than 12 km away from the harbour. The side routes provide the mixture of rural and wilderness surroundings that make this area such a joy to cycle.

Main Route

Road

distance:	46 km; circuit
terrain:	hills, some steep; several extended flat stretches
surface:	paved two-lane backroads, narrow or no shoulders; four-lane highway, wide shoulders
traffic:	moderate on streets; heavy to very heavy on highway

Services

bank machines:	numerous banks and businesses throughout the city
bike repairs:	several
liquor store:	several
groceries:	many large and small stores
camping:	Newcastle Island Provincial Park, several private campgrounds
hospital:	Nanaimo

My approach

This route is a series of connecting main streets that circumscribe the city. I start from the downtown area because I live there. Several of us use the route for its exercise and social value. It combines extended flat stretches and hills, so regardless of the direction followed it's a good workout. We usually make either the Black Bear Pub or Lantzville Pub our destination, offering an opportunity to socialize or perhaps conduct a little business.

Travelling back via Jingle Pot Road, we stop at the Jingle Pot Pub, particularly when hungry. If needing to make a quick trip home, we take the Island Highway. While always busy through Nanaimo, it's mostly a slight downhill grade from the north.

Were I camping in Nanaimo and planning to cycle all the routes in this chapter, I would stay at Living Forest Oceanside Campground just south of the city. All the routes are easy to access from here. Alternatively, Brannen Lake Campsites at the north end of the city is handy to the main route.

A brief history of Nanaimo

A ride through Nanaimo today reveals a booming modern city of almost seventy thousand. There is little evidence that until the 1940s this city had only one focus; coal. In fact, it mostly ignores its coal mining past, preferring instead to showcase to visitors its economic diversity and recreation potential. When I began to research Nanaimo's history I was astonished at the extent to which coal dominated this community.

The city's modern history begins in 1850 when a local Native reported to a Hudson's Bay Company official the existence of coal in the area. At the time HBC held the mineral rights to the Island. By 1853 there were five mines being worked in and around what is now the downtown core. They must have been small operations because the entire population of the town then was less than two hundred. As other seams were discovered in the surrounding area, output and the population escalated. In 1874, local mines produced 81,000 tons, by 1882 the output was 282,132 tons — an increase of 348 percent over eight years. In that year the mines employed 874 people. The town was booming. There was a railway connection to Victoria, a manufacturing sector, hotels, schools, breweries and a newspaper. The population had grown to four thousand.

By the time production peaked in the early twenties, over three thousand miners were producing 1.7 million tons a year from fifteen mines, and the population exceeded ten thousand. After this, cheaper and better quality coal was being discovered in the BC interior and the US Northwest, soon to be followed by petroleum as a growing alternative energy source.

Over the next thirty years, mine production steadily declined and wasn't replaced by any other economic activity. The potential for logging, fishing and agriculture which the area possessed in abundance, went largely ignored. While the rest of the West Coast flourished, Nanaimo languished. By 1951, when there was no longer any coal mining activity in area

Nanaimo's population was less than 7,200 — 3,000 less than it had been as far back as 1918.

Today the only noticable inheritances of our coal mining history can be found in exhibits at the museum, some street names, and the occasional construction problem associated with the kilometres of mine shafts under the city.

Boom times returned during the 1950s, this time fueled by post-war immigration, the completion of the giant Harmac pulp mill, and the election of a provincial government that emphasized highway construction and tourism. By now the city was also able to maximize its geographic proximity to Vancouver and its superb natural harbour as a hub for the distribution of goods and people throughout the Island. Its population grew to thirty thousand.

The city remained primarily a working man's town until the mid-eighties when it became the focus of an exodus to the Island for thousands of families from other parts of Canada, seeking a change in life style or retirement. At one point people were re-locating here at a rate of 250 per month. Our economy now includes a variety of primary and secondary manufacturing industries as well as tourism, retirement, business and personal services, and a large retail sector.

Living Forest Oceanside Campground (CG1)

193 sites, washrooms, showers, laundromat

If I were to run away from home, this is where I would stay. The tent sites are large and private and in a separate section from the RV sites. They overlook the ocean and the Nanaimo River estuary.

Located on Maki Rd. just off the main highway, 3 km from downtown, it is easy to miss. Turn east at Food Country, and follow your nose. The owner, Mr. Littlejohn is a longtime local resident and knowledgeable about area history.

Nanaimo Harbour (PI1)

The harbour is a federal facility, controlled and managed by the Nanaimo Harbour Commission. It is one the largest and most beautiful on the coast, and epitomizes the city's role as the "Hub City." There is a trend to changing this designation to the more glamorous "Harbour City." It is the location of the downtown business section, railyard, docks, public and private marinas, and seaplane, truck, rail, car and passenger ferry terminals.

Downtown

To the cyclist, aside from its view across the harbour, our downtown will appear small and unremarkable. Bisected by the busy Island Highway, it contains some office buildings, the old court house, a huge deserted hotel, a small retail section and several hotels and pubs. There is a great new pub, the Foundry, at the north end of the downtown core across from the foundry, with a large foyer inside the front doors for the safe storage of bikes.

The real beauty of our downtown is inaccessible to the cyclist. A wide paved path runs along the harbour edge and passes through parks, and past new retail and residential developments, part of a continuing waterfront enhancement program by the Commisssion. Cyclist are banned from this path, a city by-law I frequently disobey for its sheer stupidity. Partly because so many local cyclists also share this view, the path is policed.

Assembly Docks

A large percentage of the Island's lumber, plywood, pulp and paper is shipped from the assembly docks, located to the south of the downtown core. In a typical year this modern facility exports over a million metric tonnes of product via about two hundred ships. Many of these arrive from Asia, unload cargos of new cars at Vancouver, and then reload here for the return trip.

BC Ferries Terminal

The BC Ferries terminal at Departure Bay is the most visible evidence of Nanaimo's role as the Hub City. The terminal is the arrival and departure point of passengers and vehicles travelling to and from the mainland. These ships approximate 140 m (nearly 1.5 football fields) in length, and carry three hundred cars and over one thousand passengers. This terminal processes over 2 million vehicles a year and over 5 million passengers. After disembarking most head north on the nearby Island Highway. Ferries arrive and depart more than twenty times a day, mostly in daylight hours. We locals have memorized the ferry schedule, partly so we can remember to travel on the side streets after ferry arrivals. To relieve some of this congestion, BC Ferries is constructing an new terminal outside town, and also plans to add a pair of high speed catamarans.

Dinghy Dock Pub (Pub1)

8 Pirates Lane (753-2373)

The Dinghy Dock is attached to Protection Island, and can be reached by the Protection Island ferry, also owned by the pub's owner, Bob Banerd. Nine years ago Bob saw a market niche in serving visiting boaters and local residents, and opened the only registered floating pub in Canada.

The ferry leaves from the boat basin, near the government wharf. Bikes will be transported if there is room. Alternatively, if you are camped on Newcastle Island, let the Newcastle ferry operator know that you wish to go to the pub. If not busy, he will drop you off. Otherwise he will contact Bob to have you picked up.

Protection Island is the site of one of the more amusing events in Nanaimo's history. To celebrate the end of WWII residents set fire to the massive timber tipple at the mouth of an abandoned coal shaft. It collapsed into the shaft, and started an underground fire which smoldered for five years. It was finally extinguished by opening a channel of sea water into it.

Newcastle Island Provincial Park (CG2)

18 sites, washrooms, swimming

Newcastle Island is often referred to as Nanaimo's Stanley Park, without the traffic. It can be reached by a ferry which docks behind the Civic Arena, at the north end of the downtown core. Bicycles are permitted.

Once the site of a millstone quarry, the remains of which are still on display, the Island was owned by Canadian Pacific. In the thirties CP would conduct weekend excursions here from Vancouver. The island featured playing fields, a wading pool, and dance pavillion that headlined some of the big bands of the era.

Today it is a a playground for local residents and visiting boaters.

Newcastle has several kilometres of well-marked trails around and across it. One of these leads to the air shaft of an abandoned mine shaft, one of many that ran under the island from Nanaimo. Talk occasionally surfaces of opening one of these shafts to the public, enabling access to the island by foot.

Pipers Lagoon Park (PI3)

no camping

This is easily the prettiest of Nanaimo's many parks. On a forested outcropping into the Strait, it surrounds a sandy lagoon which dries at low tide, and provides warm summer swimming when the tide has risen.

For a short time at the turn of the century this was the site of a whaling station, dismantled a few years later when all the whales in the Strait had been exterminated. The nearby Shack Islands, designated as Crown land, are named after the squatters' shacks that adorn them, some of which are used as summer cabins by local residents.

Black Bear Pub (Pub2)

6210 Dumont Road (390-4800)

The Black Bear is owned and managed by John and Linda Wicks, who emigrated from England in the late eighties. John candidly admits they had to buy the pub to stay in Canada, having been admitted to this country under the the terms of a policy that stipulates they own their own business and employ Canadians. The Wicks had never managed a pub before. John is a jeweller by trade.

The Black Bear is a very relaxing pub. The Wicks don't see much difference between being a jeweller and publican. Both entail treating customers as friends, an attitude adapted by all the staff.

In the English tradition, the pub was named after a local occurrence, in this case a bear that had recently startled a local resident. The Black Bear is surrounded by fields, and the Wicks will let the needy camper tent here.

Brannen Lake Campsites (CG2)

61 sites, washrooms, showers, swimming

Brannen Lake Campsites is an easy cycle from the main highway, and adjoins a working farm which is owned by the same family.

North End (PI4)

To some like myself this point of interest will be more appropriately a point of disinterest. But if you need a shopping fix, this is where to get it. During its recent extended growth spurt Nanaimo's residential areas have spread north, and in the process spawned one of the highest ratios of per capita retail space in Canada. Much of this is in the North End.

Woodgrove Centre and the adjoining properties contain a concentration of retail outlets that lure shoppers from as far away as Port Hardy.

Lantzville Village Pub (Pub3)

7197 Lantzville Road (390-4019)

This pub was built in 1925 to provide a "better class of accommodation to the miners." It was owned by the Caillet family for the first fifty-six years, when it was remembered for the diversity of animals kept on the premises, including a deer, goats, monkey, raccoon, cow and a thieving crow.

While the building has been renovated several times over the years, the owners have always preserved the style of the original architecture. In 1979 a 115-year-old antique bar from Missoula, Montana was added. It contains two bullet holes.

I estimate that this pub has more televisions per seat than any in BC, a feature that has always mystified me because they are mostly ignored by the clientele. My attention inevitably turns to the nautical paintings on the wall — some of which are so detailed you can almost hear them.

This pub also serves a very popular Sunday brunch. Get there early because the pub fills quickly for this event.

Jingle Pot Pub (Pub4)

2211 Jingle Pot Road (753-4223)

If this trip is starting to look like a pub crawl, that may be because it frequently is, and the Jingle Pot is a popular spot. One is best to arrive here hungry. This pub has one of the most diverse menus and and serves some of the largest portions I have encountered. Fish and chips are the house specialty.

The manager also provided me with an explanation of the name, which is printed on the pub's menu.

There is more than one version as to how the name jingle pot came about. One story is that when the miners wanted to come to the surface, they would jingle a pot full of stones which was suspended on a tripod situated at the entrance of the mine shaft. Attached to the pot handle was a long rope the length of the mine shaft, and when the rope was pulled the pot swung back and forth causing the stones in the pot to "jingle," the signal to the hoist man to haul up the coal car.

Another version was that the miners would tell their wives that there would be a "jingle" in the pot tonight, meaning that today would be a big payday. Since the coin was kept in a pewter teapot (for safe keeping) the pot would jingle."

Side Route — Gabriola Island

distance:	33 km; circuit (excludes road to Drumbeg Park, 2 km one way)
terrain:	long hills, some of which are steep; few flat stretches
surface:	paved two-lane, narrow or no shoulders (road to Drumbeg Park is gravel surfaced)
traffic:	light

This is a popular daytrip for Nanaimo cyclists. Because the route is hilly it's a great workout, and for a break there is a park and pub conveniently located at about the halfway point.

The island is reached by the Gabriola Ferry, which has its own wharf at the south end of the Nanaimo downtown core. When disembarking on Gabriola I recommend waiting in the parking lot for the traffic to disperse. The hill which faces you is long, steep and narrow. Also resist the urge to enter the White Hart Pub until your return. This pub serves superb seafood chowder, but I wouldn't want to try cycling up the hill after ingesting a bowl of it.

At the top of the hill, keep right on South Road. By travelling the circuit in this direction you will avoid Brickyard Hill, the only hill in this book that has ever beaten me. It's short but very, very steep.

At the tip of the island there are two great spots to rest. One is Drumbeg Provincial Park (no camping), a sheltered bay with picnic tables and a sandstone beach. If you relish some excitement, trying building a small fire on the sandstone. We did and were surprised by plates of rock exploding into the air. We had inadvertently launched these by heating to its boiling point the water trapped in this porous rock, and creating steam eager to escape its confines.

The other rest spot is the Silva Bay Pub, located at the site of an old shipyard used to build landing craft for WWII. This pub has two personalities. In summer it is filled with boisterous boaters who visit from the attached marina. In the winter it reverts to the locals, a much quieter bunch.

Should you wish to camp on the Island, I recommend Page's Resort and Marina. This privately owned facility has ten large sites set in an old orchard, washrooms and showers. It is always quiet and in the evenings you can wander down to the docks and view the boats anchored in the harbour. The owners will also be pleased to direct you to the short-cut to Silva Bay, only a brief cycle away.

Side Route — Yellow Point

distance:	57 km; circuit (excludes Hemer Park to Boat Harbour, 5 km one way)
terrain:	rolling hills, some flat stretches (Hemer Park to Boat Harbour is flat)
surface:	paved two-lane, narrow or no shoulders; (dirt trail to Boat Harbour)
traffic:	light (none on the trail to Boat Harbour)

More often than not I ride only the portion of this route that gets me to the Crow and Gate, which is about 16 km from my home. However about once a year I go on a fitness kick, usually motivated by Moddle beating me at squash, an event roughly akin to the Second Coming. The route winds through farms and acreages and contains little traffic.

I recommend diverting through Hemer Provincial Park (no camping). The trail along the lake becomes an abandoned railway bed past the park boundary. This leads to Boat Harbour. Now deserted, this was once a coal terminal where mine output was brought by train and loaded onto ships. There is much evidence of coal here, and the footings of some old structures. There is a sheltered indentation at the end of the point that we often use for picnics.

Crow and Gate Pub (Pub5)

2313 Yellow Point Road (722-3731)

If you only visit one pub in the Nanaimo area, make it the Crow and Gate. Set on a large shaded property that includes lawns, blooming plants and a duck pond, this pub was designed to replicate the "ideal" English pub. Its designer and builder patterned the pub after his favourite pubs in southern England. The warmth and casual comfort inside are enhanced by an outside courtyard and garden.

The Crow and Gate was BC's first licensed neighbourhood pub. It's unique setting prompted the government to create new regulations to accommodate this concept. The owners, the Olson family, also pride themselves on the pub's food which is home-made on premises, without a deep fryer, TV's, and loud music and language, just don't fit.

The Olson family is pleased to have visiting cyclists camp here.

Side Route — Nanaimo Lakes

distance:	61 km; circuit
terrain:	rolling hills, flat at Nanaimo Lakes
surface:	paved two-lane, mostly without shoulders
traffic:	light

This route is a gradual uphill pull into logging country that was originally opened up by rail. The old railbed on the north side of the river is still accessible. Unfortunately, to control use by vandals it has been ditched, and some of the trestles dismantled, eliminating the possibility of using it as a cycle route to the lakes.

Upon entering the lakes region, which is still actively logged, the cyclist will encounter a gate manned by an attendant who will record your presence and charge a small user fee. The forestry company maintains a day-use area and some primitive lakeside campsites on First Lake, and requests a fee to offset clean-up and security costs. He also provides a detailed map of the area. I have explored most of the logging roads in the area and recommend doing so from a base at the First Lake campground.

The return route passes the turnoff to the Mount Benson lookout, accessible by cycle (I recommend a guide for first-time visitors) from which one can overlook all Nanaimo, and some of the Gulf Islands.

Nanaimo/Coombs/Port Alberni

The Hump

The first half of this route I have cycled many times. For years our group from Nanaimo has taken daytrips to Coombs and back. It's a training workout that combines extended flat stretches with long, steady uphills and downhills, and can be covered at a faster-than-average touring speed. The balance of the route into Port Alberni I have cycled only once, but driven frequently, so it's familiar to me.

Because much of the route is on the Island's two busiest highways, 19 and 4, traffic is frequently heavy and of every conceivable type, including logging trucks. Part is only two-lane, and can get a little frightening between Cameron Lake and Port Alberni, where it is twisting and sometimes shoulderless. There is one memorable hill, which reaches an altitude of 435 m and traverses the slope of Mount Arrowsmith and drops into Port Alberni. This is "The Hump."

Stops of interest en route include Coombs, a community that has to be seen to be believed, and Cathedral Grove, in which grow some of the world's largest trees. The Alberni Valley itself is a destination which the cyclist could easily spend several days exploring. This chapter provides a far from complete account and I strongly recommend visiting the Travel Infocentre for information on other routes and sights.

Main Route

Road

distance: 77 km; linear

terrain: combination of flat stretches and long rolling hills; long steep hills at Nanoose and entering Port Alberni

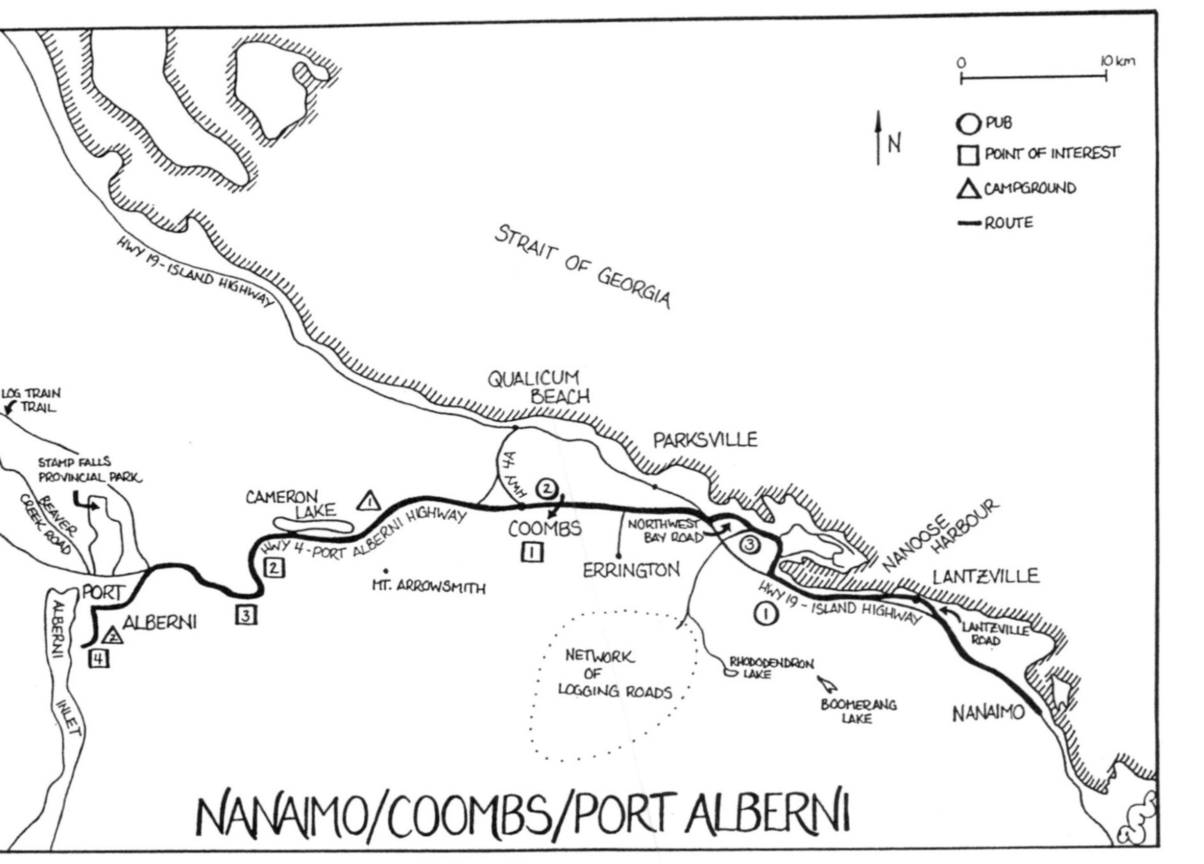
0
10 km
N
PUB
POINT OF INTEREST
CAMPGROUND
ROUTE
STRAIT OF GEORGIA
HWY 19 - ISLAND HIGHWAY
QUALICUM BEACH
PARKSVILLE
LOG TRAIN TRAIL
STAMP FALLS PROVINCIAL PARK
BEAVER CREEK ROAD
CAMERON LAKE
HWY 4A
HWY 4 - PORT ALBERNI HIGHWAY
COOMBS
NORTHWEST BAY ROAD
ERRINGTON
NANOOSE HARBOUR
LANTZVILLE
MT. ARROWSMITH
PORT ALBERNI
ALBERNI INLET
NETWORK OF LOGGING ROADS
RHODODENDRON LAKE
BOOMERANG LAKE
LANTZVILLE ROAD
NANAIMO
NANAIMO/COOMBS/PORT ALBERNI

surface:	paved four-lane, wide shoulders; paved two-lane, varying width shoulders
traffic:	moderate to heavy; buses and commercial vehicles

Services

bank machines:	Nanaimo, Port Alberni, and businesses en route
bike repairs:	Nanaimo, Port Alberni
liquor store:	Nanaimo, Port Alberni
groceries:	Nanaimo, Port Alberni, Coombs, other stores en route
camping:	Little Qualicum Falls Provincial Park, Dry Creek Park Public Campground, many public and private sites
hospital:	Nanaimo, Port Alberni

My approach

This route can be done in one day or two.

To reach Port Alberni in one day, the fastest and surprisingly most comfortable route is the Island Highway to the Port Alberni turnoff. Although the highway can get busy, it is four-lane to the turnoff and several kilometres beyond, and the shoulders are wide. Coombs is an interesting spot for a break. The remainder of the trip can also be accomplished at a reasonable pace, except for The Hump. There is a beach and freshwater swimming at Cameron Lake.

Dry Creek Municipal Campground in downtown Port Alberni is an almost wilderness setting with quick access to town, and the wharf where the Lady Rose docks.

The more leisurely two-day trip provides the opportunity to leave the highway on extensive stretches of secondary road at Lantzville and Nanoose, and camp at Little Qualicum Falls Provincial Park.

Arlington Inn (Pub1)

At the Nanoose turnoff (468-7013)

I have included this pub for its sentimental value, having visited it so often the staff knows me by name. It is a turnaround point on short daytrips and a natural stop when travelling back from Coombs, or up-Island. In fact I can truthfully claim that I have never cycled past this pub when heading south.

The pub, which recently celebrated its fiftieth anniversary, is unremarkable except for its clientele, who never seems to change between visits. Good ole boys and loggers, identified by red suspenders worn outside their shirts. Regardless of what time of the day I arrive, they are always there ahead of me, and look like they've been there for a while.

Coombs (PI1)

If at first glimpse Coombs appears a little bizarre, that's because it is — and by design. The village places no restrictions on commercial development, with the result that it has become an eclectic mix of businesses and attractions sure to stop travellers in their tracks, which happens often. The parking lots are frequently filled, and visitors are forced to park on the side of the highway, which runs past the edge of town.

For many years Coombs' dominant landmark was the Country Market, a frontier-style building with a living thatched roof on which resides a family of goats. The building itself contains a well-stocked deli, imported gifts and "stuff", and a popular ice cream counter.

Other "attractions" include the Emporium, a sort of large wood boutique barn, a pink stucco somewhat surreal strip mall, and a fake sternwheeler with a mini-golf course attached. You really have to see this village to believe it. Everyone here has a lot of fun.

Leaving Coombs on the way to Port Alberni is the Country Pies bakery. If I'm going to be camping at Little Qualicum Falls Provincial Park I stop in here and buy a couple of their melton mobray pies or sausage rolls for supper.

Frontiersman Pub (Pub2)

2280 Alberni Highway (248-9832)

People who live in Coombs, by virtue of living there, march to a different drummer. Years ago the residents of Coombs rejected government by the nearby regional district, and they manage their community by themselves, meaning by-laws are kept to a minimum. The community's eclectic collection of adults, all independent spirits, gathers at the Frontiersman.

The building itself is a unique log construction that was expanded into a pub twenty years ago, after first being a gas station, general store and restaurant. Because the walkways around the pub are busy, particularly in the summer, we generally park our bikes in a graveled area beside the back door. The owners also permit storing them on the bandstand, just inside that door.

Little Qualicum Falls Provincial Park (CG1)

94 campsites, washrooms, swimming, waterfalls

Straddling the Little Qualicum River, this campground has two levels. The lower level beside the river is the more scenic. The upper has flush toilets. I prefer the upper. Hikers will appreciate the network of trails through the surrounding forest.

Although large, this park does fill up sometimes in the summer. In the off-season the lower level is closed but accessible by bike, facilitating secluded riverside camping. However we learned first hand that the park's management frowns on this practice.

Cathedral Grove(PI2)

Cathedral Grove is one of the last accessible old-growth forests in BC. "The King of Cathedral Grove," an eight-hundred-year-old Douglas fir, is 76 m high, 3.2 m in diameter, and 9 m in circumference, about the distance of six adults holding hands.

The Hump (PI3)

The Hump is the only hill in this book that I have designated a Point of Interest. It is a 200 m rise from Cathedral Grove, and on the other side drops 435 m to sea level. It is such a dominant geographical presence that it separates weather fronts. I have often travelled to Port Alberni on business to find the wind, skies and temperature completely different from that on the Nanaimo side.

The Hump so intimidates cyclists that I tried it this year for only the first time. It helped to take a couple of rests on the way up - there is room at the roadside to do so. At the peak is a rest area where trucks are required to stop and check their brakes; the descent is a long sleigh ride, so cyclists should do the same. Braking efficiency is enhanced by removing any slack from brake cables. In our group knowledge of this technique seems to be the exclusive domain of men. If you are female, and don't have a guy handy, just turn counterclockwise those two little "screwy" things located where the brake cable enters the lever assembly housing. Remember to lock the adjustment in place by turning the inside ring clockwise back to its original position.

Port Alberni (PI4)

A city of approximately 30,000, Port Alberni bills itself as the forestry capital of Canada and the salmon capital of the world. Forty percent of the community's basic income is dependent on the forestry sector. Three hundred commercial fishboats and countless sport boats operate from the harbour, which accounts for about 20 percent of BC's commercial catch.

MacMillan Bloedel, now an international forest products giant, got its start here. Its three mills, which produce lumber, plywood, pulp, paper and newsprint, all mainly for export to Japan, dominate the city's shoreline. In 1993 the mills employed twenty eight hundred Port Alberni residents.

Port Alberni supports a remarkably well stocked and staffed Infocentre, even by the high standards of the genre. Located at the entrance to town just off Highway 4, I recommend visiting to learn more about this fascinating community.

Dry Creek Park Public Campground (CG2)

52 sites, washrooms, showers, reasonably priced

This attractive municipal campground is located right downtown in a wooded ravine. It is an ideal base from which to explore the city, and the surrounding countryside.

On my most recent trip I had it pretty well to myself. The Port Alberni region enjoys North America's highest concentration of cougars, and a few days previously there had been a rare but fatal attack on an off-road cyclist. That evening as I was preparing for bed I heard the noise of something falling from the top of the ravine behind me. Having hesitantly decided to investigate, I discovered at its base a man cradling an injured woman in his lap. I summoned the police and an ambulance, which rushed the woman to hospital — her injuries proved to be quite serious. The police interviewed the man and subsequently informed me that they had fallen into the ravine while making love. One officer volunteered that this was the strangest ending to that particular act that he had ever seen.

Side Route — Northwest Bay Road Logging Roads

Road

distance:	various
terrain:	hills, some flat stretches
surface:	two-lane or less, loose gravel, dusty
traffic:	light, mostly logging trucks and pick-ups

A short distance west of the traffic light is the administrative office of MacMillan Bloedel's Northwest Bay division. The staff there provides a map of the logging roads and designates those which are active. "Active" is a euphemism for massive off-road trucks bulging with logs and driven by impatient operators who don't give a damn whether cyclists live or die. Camping is discouraged here due to the threat of fires to the forest inventory. The roads are loose gravel and some are not maintained, so off-road tires are recommended. The forest is full of wildlife, including cougar, elk, deer and bears — the latter having been known to chase the odd cyclist. When first exploring here, I recommend a guide.

Rhododendron Lake

An energetic near-vertical climb to this small lake reveals one of North America's few wild rhododendron groves. First discovered by Mac-Blo while forest harvesting, the corporation has preserved the grove and gone so far as to add trails, benches, and plaques which identify the many other trees and plants in the grove.

Here also grow the largest salal berries I have seen. Salal is a bush which thrives in our forests. The foliage is used by florists in flower arrangements. Its berries resemble a slightly hairy concord grape. At maturity in late summer they are delicious. Bears love them.

Boomerang Lake

Named for its shape, this lake is a popular trout fishing spot.

Mount Arrowsmith

Several years ago I developed an interest in finding the logging road backroutes to Coombs, which I had previously only accessed from Highway 4. I knew it could be done, because Andrew said so. A peek at the map revealed that at least part of the route would entail some elevation because it crossed the base of Mount Arrowsmith. A series of failures without a single success transformed this interest to an obsession, which I was careful to involve my friends in.

We travelled straight up for hours on what we estimated was a parallel route to the highway, in search of the elusive Coombs connector. We never found it but were informed during a chance encounter with a couple of Natives that we were well on our way to Port Alberni. The trip back down was pretty wild. Moddle's bike broke down, a consequence of it not being designed for this type of riding, and I subsequently had to replace a $250 rear wheel. The rims had literally erased from the continuous downhill braking on this and previous attempts. And Moddle had to buy a new bike because I refused to cycle with him again until he owned one that could cope with the terrain.

We later tried a different route so steep that it involved mostly pushing our bikes uphill for hours. Again no luck, and again no idea where we were, except that it was high. On a return visit the next week in my 4X4, I noticed that we could easily see the BC ferries travelling up the Strait of Georgia from Tsawwassen.

Rocking Horse Pub (Pub3)

2038 Sanders Road, Nanoose Bay (468-7631)

This is a convenient pub to visit after cycling the Northwest Bay logging roads, or en route to or from Nanaimo by the Northwest Bay Road side road.

The Rocking Horse Pub is a ranch house. Its sixty acres were pioneered in the 1880s, and a subsequent owner used it to raise and train race horses. The house was converted to a pub in the seventies, but the property is still an active ranch, as evidenced by the surrounding pastures and barns.

Manager Doug Adair has focused the pub toward couples seeking an evening of dining, live entertainment, and dancing to country music.

Side Route — The Log Train Trail

Road

distance:	43 km; circuit
terrain:	extended flat stretches, a few short hills
surface:	abandoned railway bed; paved two-lane backroads, limited shoulders
traffic:	cycling, horse riding and hiking only on the railway bed; light on the backroads

The Log Train Trail, now designated a regional park, is the dream of Frank Stini. At one time this twenty kilometres of abandoned railway bed was the preferred method of hauling logs harvested to the nearby Alberni Inlet. Frank, who has been hiking the trail since 1957, made its restoration a retirement project. Enlisting the cooperation of the Port Alberni Equine Society, volunteers, and government youth grants, the old grade was cleared and prepared for its present use by hikers, equestrians, and cyclists.

The route, which passes through second-growth forest and farmland, also includes the sites of two former mills. One, McLean's Sawmill is a National Historic Site and is being re-constructed to demonstrate a working mill of its era. Complete details of the Log Train Trail are contained in a brochure available from the Infocentre, located near where the route begins.

When we cycled this route we began on the railway grade at its Highway 4 end, travelled to its end at Woolsey Road, and then returned via the backroads, most of the time on Beaver Creek Road. This presented the chance to visit Stamp Falls Provincial Park which features a waterfall and fish ladder where one can view migrating ascending salmon.

Ucluelet/Tofino via Alberni Inlet

Sleeping Beauty

Residents of the Island refer to this area simply as "the west coast," or Long Beach, for the sixteen kilometresof beach that is its most outstanding landmark. The west coast can be reached by Highway 4, or by the MV *Lady Rose*, a working coastal freighter which sails between Port Alberni and several destinations, including Ucluelet.

The trip entails a half-day sea voyage, followed by a mostly flat stretch of paved highway with reasonably wide shoulders. It connects two coastal communities, Ucluelet and Tofino, and passes through Pacific Rim National Park, one of Canada's most beautiful and most popular national parks.

This "ride" is most memorable for its scenery — fjords, coastal rain forest, mountains and beaches — spectacular, even by Island standards. The area also abounds in wildlife. Seals, sea lions and eagles can be viewed year-round, with bear, whale and even the occasional cougar sighting possible. The national park campground at Green Point contains the highest density of raccoons we have ever encountered.

Note: I do not recommend cycling the highway from Port Alberni to the coast. While it is entirely paved and scenic, several stretches contain narrow or no shoulders and nearly blind curves. Having driven it for years and observed the effects of this terrain on incautious and unskilled drivers, sometimes behind the wheels of semi-trailers and large recreational vehicles, I would never attempt to cycle it.

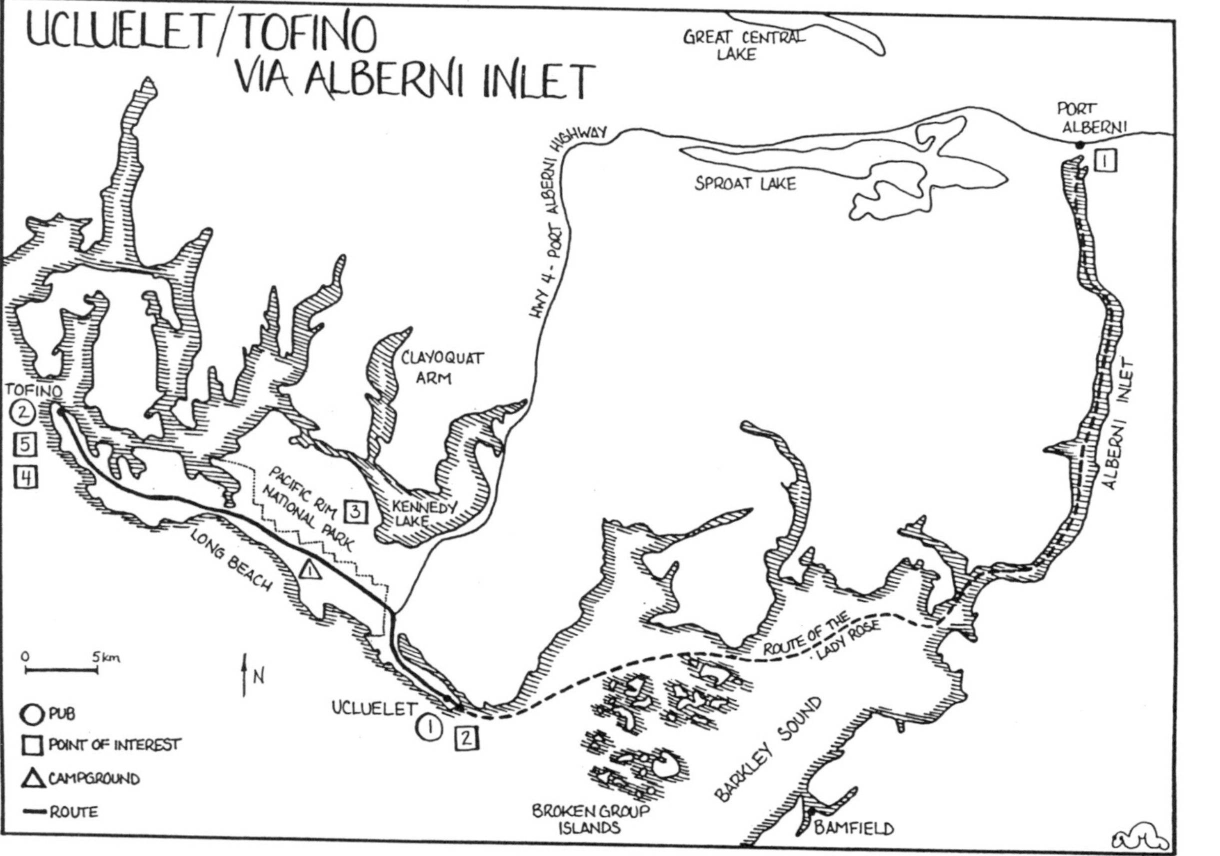
UCLUELET/TOFINO
VIA ALBERNI INLET
GREAT CENTRAL LAKE
PORT ALBERNI
1
SPROAT LAKE
HWY 4 - PORT ALBERNI HIGHWAY
CLAYOQUAT ARM
TOFINO
2
5
4
ALBERNI INLET
PACIFIC RIM NATIONAL PARK
3
KENNEDY LAKE
LONG BEACH
ROUTE OF THE LADY ROSE
0
5km
N
UCLUELET
1
2
BARKLEY SOUND
PUB
POINT OF INTEREST
CAMPGROUND
ROUTE
BROKEN GROUP ISLANDS
BAMFIELD

Main Route

Road

distance:	45 km; linear
terrain:	mostly flat stretches, a few rolling hills
surface:	calm, with a possibility of swells after leaving the Inlet; paved road, two-lane — adequate shoulders; paved parallel pedestrian trail just before Tofino
traffic:	light to moderate

Services

bank machines:	Ucluelet, Tofino
bike repairs:	Tofino (limited services), Port Alberni
liquor store:	Ucluelet, Tofino
groceries:	Ucluelet, Tofino
camping:	Pacific Rim National Park, numerous private sites
hospital:	Tofino

My approach

This trip is best taken in late spring, summer or early fall. During this period the *Lady Rose* (or the MV *Francis Barkley*, an alternate vessel) runs her scheduled excursions to Ucluelet. During the other months the west coast days are cold, wet and short — not the stuff of which pleasant holidays are made. It is a comfortable one-day trip with ample time for sightseeing. The *Lady Rose* is boarded in the morning at the Argyle Pier in Port Alberni, a few minutes cycle from the Dry Creek Park municipal campsite. The boat docks in Ucluelet at lunch time.

If planning to camp at Green Point, by far the most desirable and busy campground on the route, and you have not made a reservation, go straight there. Sites are rented on a first-come, first-served basis and there is no overflow area for hikers or bikers. I found this out the hard way after taking time for lunch at Ucluelet, and arriving at Green Point to find it full.

Once settled into a site the cyclist can pursue a series of options including exploring the park and its beaches, cycling to Tofino for its numerous attractions and tours, or returning to sightsee in Ucluelet.

The return route to Port Alberni can be accomplished by bus (there is a tour company associated with the *Lady Rose*), or by boat.

MV Lady Rose (PI1)

Built in Scotland in 1937, the *Lady Rose* has room for a hundred passengers. While a popular tourist attraction from June to October, its original and continuing role is that of work boat. It is the main connection to civilization for some of the camps, and residences along the inlet, delivering mail, passengers and supplies. On my trip, in addition to cyclists was a group of kayakers destined for the Broken Group Islands, an archipelago at the mouth of the Inlet which is also part of Pacific Rim National Park.

The crew gladly assists with the loading and unloading of bicycles, and reasonably priced cooked breakfasts and lunches are served in the ship's galley.

On my trip, taken late in June, I found my attention divided between the scenery, my fellow passengers, and my fellow passengers reaction to the scenery. The scenery is a moving backdrop of forest, mountains, inlets, the occasional dwelling, wildlife, and sport fishermen reeling in salmon. The skipper announces items of interest to passengers on a public address system. At one point the ship changed course to provide a better view of a black bear feeding at the shore. While we saw no whales on this trip, there had been regular sightings during the previous weeks.

On the boat trip I met a French woman, who cycled from Idaho on her way to Alaska. She approached me because we both had Giant bikes and she had a mechanical problem, a broken spoke. Her predicament brought to mind two lessons. First, she had broken some spokes a couple of weeks earlier and only replaced the broken ones. Spokes tend to wear out uniformly; if one goes it is advisable to replace them all. Secondly, the west coast is no place for a defective bike. The nearest reliable repair store is in Port Alberni.

Ucluelet (PI2)

"Ucluelet" means "safe landing place." It was a safe place for the Nuu-Chah-Nulth people to land their huge canoes and build their homes. In the 1880s it was a centre for fur sealers. The village now boasts the third-largest fish catch tonnage in BC. A ride through the harbour area reveals several fish processing plants, some with retail outlets. While none formally offer tours, with a little luck at least a quick peek inside may be possible.

Of the two communities on this route, Ucluelet most accurately reflects life in a west coast village before tourism became popular. Employment for the year-round population of two thousand is still derived principally from logging and the fishery, with tourism a distant third. This is a working man's town, unpretentious and comfortable.

While in Ucluelet I recommend a visit to an example of a disappearing part of Canada's maritime heritage — the staffed Coast Guard Station. Amphitrite Point marks the entrance to Ucluelet harbour, on a notorious stretch of coast once known as the "Graveyard of the Pacific." Constructed on a rugged outcropping and linked by a foot path, it contains a search light, bellowing fog horn and electronic surveillance equipment which monitors busy Pacific ship traffic.

Eagle's Nest Marine Pub (Pub1)

140 Bay Street, Ucluelet (726-7570)

The Eagle's Nest is a new pub just a short cycle from where the *Lady Rose* docks. Located on the harbour front it has been designed to optimize watching the comings and goings of the pleasure and commercial fleets. The property has been in owner Norm Reite's family for years. When he commissioned the design if the new building, he incorporated the wishes of his clientele, which included a view of the harbour.

The pub capitalizes on its location by specializing in fresh seafood, with a "catch of the day" that can include snapper, halibut, salmon, sole, clams or oysters.

Pacific Grey Whales

Hunted nearly to extinction earlier in the century, these huge but gentle mammals now number nearly twenty thousand. They can reach lengths of fifty feet, and weigh nearly forty tons. Each year they migrate up the west coast of North America to the Bering Sea from their winter feeding and mating grounds in the Baja. Pregnant females, adult males and juveniles leave first, followed in several weeks by the cows and their calves. For unknown reasons a pod of forty or so remains off our west coast year round.

Grey whales can be identified by their distinctive water spouts as they empty their lungs after surfacing. They are most numerous in this area between February and June. With diligence, and binoculars they can be spotted from shore. Alternatively, numerous whale sighting tours originate in Ucluelet and Tofino.

Pacific Rim National Park (PI3)

Established in 1971, Pacific Rim is Canada's first national park. It comprises three units. The West Coast Trail, which has been described in "Cowichan Lake, Our Logginng Past"; the Broken Group, a paddlers paradise; and the Long Beach unit, located between Ucluelet and Tofino. It is estimated that these three units combined host a million visitors annually.

The Long Beach unit, on which there is considerable free information at Tourist Infocentres, includes in its attractions:

- Five beaches, four of them contiguous, and all accessible by trails.
- Eight designated hiking trails, one to the remains of a turn-of-the-century placer gold mining operation.
- Radar Hill, a former WWII radar installation with a panoramic view of Clayoquot Sound.
- Wickaninnish Centre, an interpretive centre exploring the natural and cultural history of the area.

The beaches, which I lack the literary skills to describe adequately, hold an almost mystical attraction. I have friends, my wife included, who periodically feel compelled to drive there for the day and just sit, watch the waves roll in and be alone with their thoughts.

Green Point (CG1)

90 sites, washrooms, swimming, surfing, and wind sailboarding; reservations recommended: 1-800-663-6000

In the summer this is undoubedly the Island's busiest campground. Before the recently implemeted reservation system campers would wait for days at private sites for their turn to register at Green Point. This is also one of the Island's most beautiful campgrounds. The sites are large, private and perfectly maintained by park personnel. And of course there is the beach, a short descent down a bluff from the campground.

The beach is ideal for hiking, sealife watching and sun bathing. The sand is sufficiently firm a metre or so above the water line to support cycling on bikes with wide tires. The water itself is pretty chilly, but not enough to prevent kids and some hardy adults from enjoying it. I briefly tried the swimming a few years ago, but quit in deference to retaining my bass voice. The surfers wear wet suits.

Tofino (PI4)

Tofino, a village just slightly larger than Ucluelet, is at the other end of Long Beach and is remarkably different. Here, tourism is king and there is a profusion of craft shops, art galleries, tour outfitters and other visitor services. While not a "typical" west coast village, Tofino demonstrates the importance of tourism to this region.

The cycling camper's first exposure to Tofino occurs shortly after leaving the national park. There, if still in need of a campsite, one is presented with a string of private campgrounds, all offering sites at or near a

Long Beach near Tofino — Pacific Rim National Park

beach. Especially in the summer, these sites can be quite expensive and often fully booked. Plan to arrive before noon.

Roy Vickers' Eagle Aerie Gallery (PI5)

350 Campbell Street, Tofino (1-800-663-0669)

Roy Vickers, a world-renowned artist, has made his home in Tofino since the 1980s. His unique style of serigraphs captures the mystical beauty of the west coast and the spirituality of his Native heritage. His gallery has been designed as a traditional long house in which he displays his art and that of a protégé, Ed Hill. Admission is free and the visitor can purchase framed and unframed limited editions, prints and, for $50,000 or so, an original.

Blue Heron Inn (Pub2)

Weigh West Resort, 634 Campbell Street, Tofino (725-3277)

This is another pub with a great view. The building is free-standing on pillars over Tofino harbour, and looks across to Meares Island. There is always something happening outside its windows, including the passing of eagles, blue herons and the occasional whale.

The pub also faces toward Clayoquot Sound, recently the site of confrontations between loggers and environmentalists resulting in demostrations, civil disobedience, and mass convictions that focussed worldwide attention to the plight of BC's old-growth forests. It also helped influence forest management legislation.

Comox Valley

Beach Country

When travelling this route I'm used to seeing hundreds of boats, commercial and sport, fishing for salmon in the Strait of Georgia. Today they were gone, because this year for the first time in memory there were no salmon to catch. This route symbolizes the importance of the ocean to the Island. I am grateful to Kip Slater, friend and retired federal fisheries officer, for his assistance with this chapter.

Unlike the other routes that I revisited to prepare this book, this one I anticipated with some reservation due to the traffic. North of Parksville and south of Courtenay the highway narrows to mostly two-lane, often with very narrow shoulders. Because this is the only route between these communities, it is jammed with traffic of every description, all moving at highway speed. A four-lane highway is currently under construction just inland of the Island Highway that is projected to relieve this pressure. This section is scheduled for completion in 1996–97, and could transform this route into a pleasant, ocean-side cycle.

If able to ignore the traffic — probably not a safe idea — the cycling is easy, long open flat stretches and rolling hills. Consequently the prevailing wind direction here, more than on some other routes, can be a major help or hindrance.

This is prime tourist country. The beaches, ocean, and warm dry climate attract thousands every year and support an extensive tourism and hospitality infrastructure. The area's geography and, until recently, reasonably priced real estate, have combined to make it a popular retirement destination. While communities on the route are still small by urban standards, they have grown at an annual rate of nearly 10 percent.

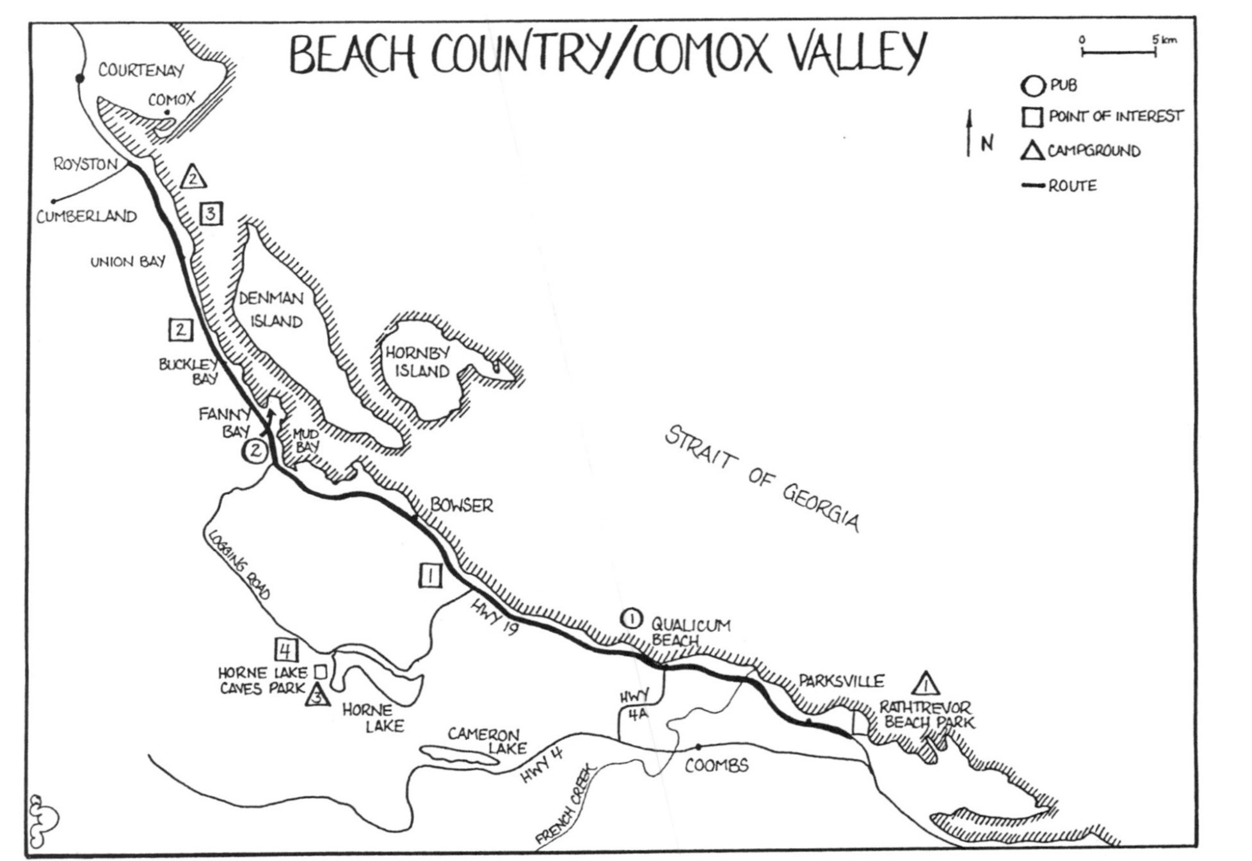

BEACH COUNTRY/COMOX VALLEY
0
5 km
PUB
POINT OF INTEREST
CAMPGROUND
ROUTE
N
COURTENAY
COMOX
ROYSTON
CUMBERLAND
UNION BAY
DENMAN ISLAND
HORNBY ISLAND
BUCKLEY BAY
FANNY BAY
MUD BAY
BOWSER
STRAIT OF GEORGIA
LOGGING ROAD
HWY 19
QUALICUM BEACH
HORNE LAKE CAVES PARK
HORNE LAKE
CAMERON LAKE
HWY 4A
HWY 4
FRENCH CREEK
COOMBS
PARKSVILLE
RATHTREVOR BEACH PARK

Main Route

Road

distance:	68 km; linear
terrain:	long flat stretches; rolling hills, some long
surface:	paved two-lane, shoulders of varying widths
traffic:	moderate to heavy

Services

bank machines:	all population centres, and some businesses in between
bike repairs:	Parksville, Qualicum Beach, Courtenay
liquor store:	Parksville, Qualicum Beach, Bowser, Courtenay
groceries:	numerous en route
camping:	Rathtrevor Beach Provincial Park, many private sites
hospital:	Nanaimo, Comox

My approach

If not planning a detour to Hornby and Denman islands, I recommend cycling the route in one day. After a while the sights acquire a certain sameness to them, resulting in sightseeing of the "cycle by" type, rather than stopping. Continuous vehicle noise in the left ear becomes tedious, which also prompts wanting to complete the route in a day.

In addition to the pubs I have mentioned, the Crown and Anchor in Bowser is a convenient mid-route break.

Rathtrevor Beach to the south, and Kingfisher Resort to the north are practical start and end points.

A brief history of the Strait of Georgia fishery

Less than a century ago this fishery literally teemed with salmon. There are five species of Pacific salmon on the west coast — sockeye, coho, pink, chum, and spring (chinook). They are highly valued for their taste, in Canada and internationally. Toward the end of their lives the salmon swim through the Strait from the open Pacific, where they have lived for the past two to five years, to the streams where they originated. They migrate upstream, spawn and then die, a process which can be observed in many Island rivers and streams during the autumn. The timing of these annual migrations varies by species, meaning that in years past there have been concentrations of one species or another from June through November in the Strait.

The salmon fishery has three main stakeholders, commercial, sport, and aboriginal. As recently as twenty years ago there were enough fish to go around. Commercial openings, as regulated by the federal Department of Fisheries and Oceans, were sufficient to ensure lucrative catches and still preserve the broodstock. Sport fishing thrived, with tourists arriving from all over the world confident in being able to catch large numbers of these highly edible fish. The aboriginal fishery, largely unregulated and guaranteed in our constitution, was practised without overt resentment from the non-Native community.

As a result of the declining fish population we are now faced with bankruptcies in the commercial fleet, a loss of tourism, and bitterness toward aboriginals that sometimes borders on violence. At this writing it is unclear whether 1995's disaster is an omen for the future, or just a temporary aberration. DFO data predicts a future return of larger runs.

The present confusion around the fishery is epitomized in the following statements from the Nanaimo Canada Employment Centre's quarterly *Labour Market Reviews*, which summarizes input from various economic stakeholders. In the third quarter, 1994 edition, "Local scientists maintain that our sockeye stocks are fairly healthy and there is no conservation threat, despite counting mistakes." Then, in the first quarter 1995 edition, "No one wants to repeat the calamity of last year when more than a million sockeye disappeared." In fact, by the summer of 1995, the period in which commercial fishermen derive most of their annual income, the commercial fishery was virtually closed. The number of fish caught in the few openings that were allowed barely covered the cost of fuel.

The fishery controversy is more complex because so many of the cultural and scientific ramifications are not yet fully understood.

Fish farms

If salmon catches are declining while worldwide appreciation for this fish continues, why haven't prices sky-rocketed? The answer of course is farmed fish — salmon that are grown under controlled conditions in land tanks or sea pens. The supply of these has more than offset the decline in the wild catch, and prices are often as low as they were years ago. In addition to satisfying domestic demand, farmed fish are now BC's largest agricultural export.

Rathtrevor Beach Provincial Park (CG1)

174 sites, washrooms, showers, beach, designated hiker/biker area, reservations permitted

In spite of its size, this site, once a homestead, is usually full in the summer. Fortunately this is not likely to be a concern to the cyclist. The hiker/biker area is an expansive area of lush grass surrounded on three sides by mature forest. This area, with access to both the huge beach and the park facilities, is an excellent place to stop on the road north.

Rathtrevor is an ideal location from which to explore the nearby communities of Parksville, Qualicum Beach and Coombs, a fun circular day-trip.

Shady Rest (Pub1)

Qualicum Beach (752-6667)

This little pub, wedged between the Island Highway and the beach is endearing for two reasons. It has an unsurpassed view across the Strait of Georgia, particularly on a clear, sunny day. It also serves the best deep-fried food, usually seafood, on the Island.

Big Qualicum River Fish Hatchery (PI1)

Fish hatcheries are the most obvious components in the federal government's fishery enhancement policy, a series of initiatives to preserve our salmon stock. There are several hatcheries on the Island. They are open to visitors and the roads to them well marked.

The Big Qualicum facility is one of the earliest and largest hatcheries. It manages the entire river watershed from its beginning at Horne Lake, to its mouth at the Strait of Georgia. Its purpose is to optimize natural spawning conditions by ensuring that fish have an adequate supply of water, gravel beds that are free of excessive silt, and safety from predators. This natural process is also supplemented by fry which are raised at the hatchery from eggs and milt extracted from returning salmon. This increases the overall fish population, while ensuring genetic integrity.

The staff at the hatchery also enumerates returning species. This assists in projecting returns in order to configure future commercial openings. It also provides a basis for evaluating the effectiveness of past and future conservation measures.

Fanny Bay Inn (Pub2)

Fanny Bay (335-2323)

The "FBI", as it is known locally is the most visible sign on the highway of what was once a thriving community. Fanny Bay was home to one of the largest shake mills in BC until the fifties, when it was closed due to declining prices and lack of accessible raw material. Other than the Inn, the most noticeable evidence now are some remains of the old wharves, and the water tower which supplied the whole town. If not too busy, owner Dave Hopkins is pleased to inform visitors of the town's history, and direct their attention to some of the old photographs adorning the pub's walls.

The FBI was recently voted the best pub in BC based on criteria that included ambience, decor, service and quality of fare. There are usually Harley-Davidson's parked outside, a result of the friendship between these "knights of the road" and the owner.

This is a convenient spot to await the ferry to Denman Island, which can be seen crossing Lambert Channel a couple of kilometres to the north.

Baynes Sound Oysters (PI2)

The inter-tidal waters of Baynes Sound are the location of some of the most prolific oyster farms on the west coast. To the casual observer they stand out as mounds of white shells surrounding large buildings pressed against the shoreline. I have travelled past them for years knowing only that they were oyster farms, whatever they were, and wondering why they didn't clean up their shells. Assuming that the cyclist from off-Island might be curious about these establishments, I contacted Glen Hadden, the owner of Fanny Bay Oysters, one of the largest oyster farms in BC.

Glen explained that the mounds of shells are an essential early component to growing oysters. Every second day from April to the end of August, twenty-four million microscopic oyster larvae are flown here from the United States. They are introduced into tanks that contain warm seawater and a quantity of shells. The shells are a medium to which they naturally attach. For the next five days they are pampered and fed in a controlled environment that hastens their development as sprats. During this time the water temperature in the tank is reduced to that of the surrounding Sound. The shells, with sprat attached and still only barely visible to the human eye, are then placed on racks and covered with burlap (to protect them from predators and excessive sunlight respectively) and deposited in the inter-tidal zone. In three years they mature and are harvested for domestic consumption and export.

Union Bay (PI3)

Today Union Bay is just a small collection of buildings on the other side of the highway from a small boat basin used mostly by sport fishermen to launch and haul out boats. Early this century it was one of the busiest coal ports on the coast. For over fifty years coal was transported on a twenty kilometre rail line from the collieries in Cumberland to Union Bay, from where it was shipped around the world.

Bill Maximick, a Comox Valley artist, has recreated the port at its heyday in his painting "Union Bay," a copy of which hangs in the Kingfisher pub. It records a startling contrast between then and now.

Kingfisher Oceanside Inn and RV Park (CG2)

20 sites, washrooms, showers, pool, hot tub, laundromat

Kingfisher is a departure from my usual choice of campgrounds, which values private and comfortable sites. Being an RV park, it possesses neither of these characteristics. The sites are small, barren, hard and lumpy. However they are ocean front, with a view across Comox Harbour. Campers can also access the amenities of the Inn, which include a restaurant and pub.

Kingfisher's main appeal is location. It is a day's ride to either Nanaimo or Campbell River, a convenient distance to the Powell River ferry, and a practical base from which to cycle the Cumberland, Courtenay, Comox circuit.

Side Route — Horne Lake

distance:	various
terrain:	hills, some extended low grades, others steep
surface:	logging roads
traffic:	light to very light

This route is an opportunity for some adventure, a freshwater swim and a detour from the Island Highway. As an alternative, although much longer, to the highway you can ride the logging roads from the Horne Lake turnoff, 14 km past Qualicum Beach, to Mud Bay, just south of Fanny Bay. I do not recommend this without either a guide or an accurate map. The road, while in good condition, is through dense second-growth forest, and has some confusing connecting roads. This is also cougar and bear country, with sightings and lost pets a common occurrence.

Another option is over Mount Horne into Port Alberni, a trail frequented mainly by young people in 4x4s and pick-up trucks as a short-cut between Port Alberni and the Island Highway. The route, which is steep, rocky and narrow, entails following a series of arrows drawn on paper plates attached to trees. When in doubt, believe the plates, not your eyes. The "road" crests at a hydro right-of-way, with Port Alberni and the Log Train Trail several hundred meters below.

Horne Lake Family Campground (CG3)

100 sites, swimming

This campground is located near the entrance to the provicial park. I have never stayed at this spot because my business partner has a nearby lakeshore cabin to which I have a key. It appears to be a convenient location to take a break, or from which to make camp before exploring the surrounding logging roads.

Horne Lake Caves Provincial Park (PI4)

no camping allowed

Caves terrify me, so the reader expecting a narrative on spelunking will be disappointed. Other than to peer into some of their entrances, I have never set foot in a Horne Lake cave, nor will I. " Six undeveloped caves are an impressive aspect of Vancouver Isalnd's natural heritage in this park at the west end of Horne Lake. Four caves are open to the public and anyone planning to enter should be in good physical conditon, well equipped and familiar with cave exploration safety and procedures." (Provincial Parks of Vancouver Island) Go for it.

Denman and Hornby Islands

A Boys' Trip

Every year Bill, Tom, Terry and I depart on a cycling and camping trip. Although each of us sees the other throughout the year, this is the only time we convene as a group. In 1995 we went to Hornby and Denman islands, the two most northern Gulf Islands.

These islands are reached from Vancouver Island by a short ferry ride from the Buckley Bay terminal. The ferry is scheduled, but when demand is heavy, which is much of the summer, it runs back and forth continuously.

The route can be covered easily in a day, including stopping to sightsee. The roads, while narrow, are paved and lightly travelled. There is one intimidating hill, on Denman Road just past downtown Denman. It's very steep, but not as difficult as it first appears. The rest of the trip is rolling hills and flat stretches, except for the narrow foot path between Ford's Cove and the Hornby Island ferry terminal.

The islands themselves, while geographically close, are cultural opposites. Denman is a counter-culture haven, Hornby a holiday destination for the upwardly mobile.

If you are particular about your brand of wine, buy it on Vancouver Island. The Denman Island General Store is the only outlet on the route, and its selection is limited.

Campsites are scarce in the summer, particularly on Hornby. Bradsdadsland Waterfront Camping is in my opinion the best campground on either island, but reserve well ahead. The campsite above the marina at Ford's Cove is not yet as well known as the others and usually has vacancies.

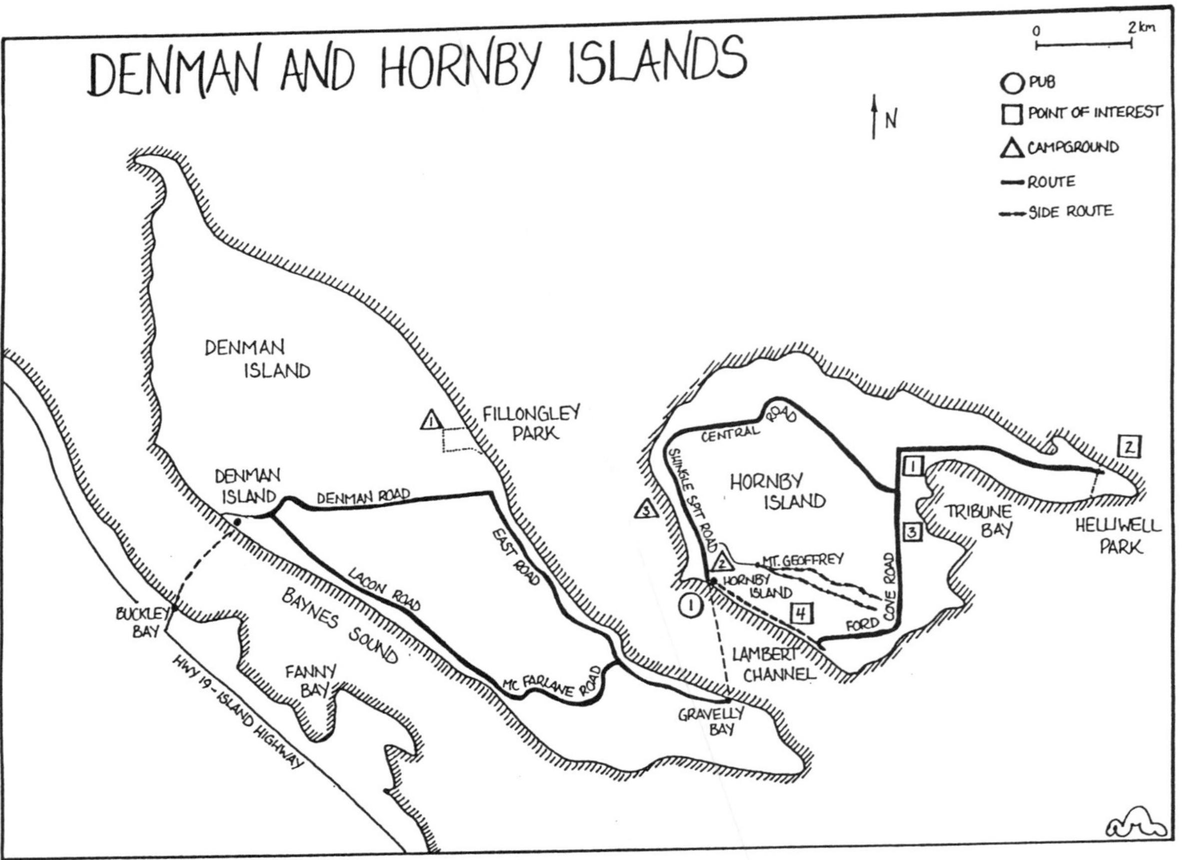
DENMAN AND HORNBY ISLANDS
0
2 km
PUB
POINT OF INTEREST
CAMPGROUND
ROUTE
SIDE ROUTE
N
DENMAN ISLAND
FILLONGLEY PARK
DENMAN ISLAND
DENMAN ROAD
EAST ROAD
LACON ROAD
MC FARLANE ROAD
BAYNES SOUND
BUCKLEY BAY
FANNY BAY
HWY 19 - ISLAND HIGHWAY
GRAVELLY BAY
LAMBERT CHANNEL
CENTRAL ROAD
SHINGLE SPIT ROAD
HORNBY ISLAND
MT. GEOFFREY
HORNBY ISLAND
FORD
COVE ROAD
TRIBUNE BAY
HELLIWELL PARK

Main Route

Road

distance:	47 km; circuit
terrain:	rolling hills, long flat stretches; one steep hill
surface:	paved two-lane, narrow or no shoulders; narrow foot path
traffic:	light

Services

bank machines:	none
bike repairs:	downtown Denman, Hornby Island beside Co-op
liquor store:	Denman Island General Store
groceries:	Denman Island General Store, Hornby Island Co-op
camping:	Fillongley Provincial Park, Bradsdadsland Waterfront Camping, limited additional private sites
hospital:	Comox

My approach

Although this is a circular route for us it has a specific destination, the beach at Tribune Bay on Hornby Island. There are a couple of routes across Denman to reach the ferry to Hornby Island. We usually start on Denman Road, thereby completing the aforementioned nasty hill while our legs are fresh, and return by Lacon Road.

When on Hornby we follow Central Road around to Ford's Cove, stopping on the way at Tribune Bay Provincial Park. Ford's Cove connects to the ferry terminal by a narrow and in places dangerous foot path which should be attempted only with a companion.

Denman Island

When disembarking from the ferry, it is essential to wait for vehicles to pass. The next stretch of road is narrow and steep.

While Denman is primarily a farming and logging community, some of its residents commute to the Comox Valley to work. Visiting Denman resembles falling into a sixties time capsule. The island is a pastoral haven for flower children of all ages. A "people watcher" will want to linger in the village above the ferry dock. I apologize for not including more text on Denman. I know it only as a pleasant ride between ferries, past farms and residences, many of which advertise crafts.

Fillongley Provincial Park (CG1)

10 sites

It is a small, treed park on the ocean front, and occupies a former homestead. The previous owner willed the land to the province for use as a park.

If I ever wanted to disappear for awhile, this would be an ideal location.

Hornby Island

By virtue I suspect of its magnificent beach, and being an additional ferry trip from Vancouver Island, Hornby is a cultural shift from Denman. While it too enjoys a representation of beaded folk, it is also home to a thriving community of artists, and a summer residence for the affluent.

For ten days every summer the island hosts The Hornby Festival, an arts festival which attracts musicians, artists, writers and dancers from across Canada. While the venue for most of the events is the island's Hall, some readings and recitals occur in private homes. The *Victoria Times-Colonist* recently referred to this event as "One of the finest, most adventurous and eclectic little festivals in the world."

The island has two personalities, one for the summer and one for the rest of the year. The summer, always warm and dry, sees thousands of happy vacationers. In the fall it returns to the serenity that one would expect of a location that is two ferry rides removed from the mainstream. On a recent visit there we learned Hornby has a seasonal population of homeless. These individuals rent the homes of the summer residents during the off-season, but are displaced by their owners during the summer. Rather than leave the island they often camp for the summer.

Thatch Pub (Pub1)

Hornby Island Resort (335-0136)

The Thatch Pub, owned by John and Karen Ross, is a unique building fortuitously located at the end of the ferry dock. The visitor will immediately notice its live thatched roof — a technique adopted by the pioneers to ensure coolness in the summer, and keep out the rain in the winter. As an added touch, this is covered with obsolete farm equipment. John and Karen, who own the entire resort, bought it in 1984 as a "five-year plan, and are still here." As a result of the resort connection, the pub's emphasizes its cuisine. During the summer it features nightly barbecues on the deck and a huge salad buffet.

The pub building is surrounded on three sides by glass, enabling guests to appreciate the view of the adjoining beach, a popular spot for beach volleyball.

Denman Island ferry dock — bikes fully loaded.

Hornby Island Resort (CG2)

10 sites, washrooms, showers, laundromat, swimming

We discovered this location by accident. We had just started up the hill after disembarking from the ferry and having a quick beer at the Thatch. Unable to reserve a spot at Bradsdadsland, we still didn't know where we were going to camp for the night. Hold it! Isn't that a campground behind that pub?

A quick U-turn and we got the last site. A pub with a campground; a campground with a pub. It was like dying and going to heaven. Does it get any better?

Hornby Island Resort has it all — beach, tennis courts, showers laundromat, view of the sun setting behind the mountains, and nightcaps. It is also the only campground I know that offers psychic readings. No kidding.

Tribune Bay Provincial Park (PI1)

Tribune Bay boasts a kilometre of fine sandy beach surrounded by hectares of parkland. Because the bay is shallow the water here is warm, and excellent for swimming. The property also contains the "remains of Hornby Island Lodge, one of the oldest and once one of the largest resorts in the Gulf Islands" (Wolferstan).

There is no camping in the park, but there are extensive day-use facilities including a well, picnic tables and shelters.

There is reportedly a nude beach south of Tribune Bay.

Helliwell Provincial Park (PI2)

Helliwell, off bounds to camping and cycling, features a five-kilometre hike around the bluffs of St. John Point. The high cliffs are an excellent vantage point for viewing marine life in the Strait of Georgia.

Not far from here is Whaling Station Bay, one hundred years ago an active whale processing centre "to render down the hundreds of sperm, humpback and bowhead whales caught in the northern straits" (Wolferstan). Needless to say, the whales were hunted to extinction.

Hornby Island Co-op (PI3)

Not just a food store, this is Hornby's social gathering place and great place to people watch, as are the adjoining kiosks which specialize in local crafts and other "stuff."

There is also a campsite behind the Co-op, with easy access to the beach at Tribune Bay. It is often crowded.

Bradsdadsland Waterfront Camping (CG3)

25 sites, washrooms, showers, laundromat

This privately owned campground sits on a ridge facing west across Lambert Channel. It is the only campground I have visited in which quiet is the law. "No music, whispers after 11 P.M." Noise of any sort is simply not tolerated, a policy emphasized at registration. This assurance is comforting and must be popular, because Bradsdadsland is frequently full.

Spit Trail (PI4)

I would be remiss in not providing an accurate description of this trail, which appears on many maps of the area to be a convenient 3.5 km short cut between Ford's Cove and the ferry dock. While most of the trail can be ridden, parts are extremely narrow and others washed out. In several places it is necessary to walk and even carry your bike.

We first attempted the trail with loaded bikes. Had I been alone I would not have reached the end. In spots the trail is so narrow and steep that two are required to manhandle a bike. The sheer drop to the ocean is also unnerving. In one such situation we encountered a solar-powered recumbent cycle coming toward us. It was being ridden by its inventor who was successfully balancing on sections of trail on which we were barely able to walk. (In fact, in retelling this story I'm beginning to wonder if I dreamt it.)

Side Route — Mount Geoffrey

distance:	various, approximately 10-15 km; circuit
terrain:	steep uphill/downhill
surface:	loose gravel and packed earth logging roads and trails
traffic:	occasional hikers and cyclists

Mount Geoffrey is a 300 m peak from which one can see across Denman to the east side of Vancouver Island. Deep Bay, Fanny Bay, and the ferry terminal at Buckley Bay are visible, as is Comox, some twenty-five kilometres to the north. It is reached via a series of old logging trails, a map of which can be purchased at the Co-op.

For our ascent we had a guide, Andre Sullivan. He is the athletic fifteen-year-old son of a business associate who maintains a summer residence on Hornby. I learned some things from Andre the morning he led us up the mountain. Specifically, no matter how hard I try to convince myself otherwise, there is a huge difference between fifteen- and forty-nine-year-old legs. Secondly, "moderately technical" means expecting at any moment to see your heart come blasting through your chest. Finally, "you will need to steer" is off-road talk for trees that are barely far enough apart to permit passage of your handle bars. Thank you, Andre.

Cumberland/Courtenay/Comox

A Figure Eight through History

The Comox Valley could easily be the destination for an entire cycling holiday. In addition to the routes described in this chapter are numerous backroads, logging roads and hiking trails. The cyclist can also tour Denman and Hornby islands and Campbell River from here in a day.

The Valley is another of Canada's fastest growing areas that is located on the Island. It contains three municipalities which are nearly adjoining, Cumberland, Courtenay and Comox. However each evolved separately, resulting in uniquely different communities. Cumberland, now a village of only two thousand, earlier this century was the second-largest coal producer on the North American west coast. Courtenay was a logging centre, and while it still retains some of that identity, is now an agricultural, tourism and recreation region. Comox began with farming and logging, then added the Canadian air force base, and recently emerged as a seaside and retirement destination.

In many ways these three towns reflect the transition of the Island as a whole. Its resource base is significantly enhanced by its tourism and recreation appeal. Expenditures by visitors to the Valley generate an estimated $75 million annually.

I recommend dedicating an entire day to the main route. This will allow extended stops at points of interest.

With the exception of Ryan Road (four-lane, wide shoulders) the route is mostly two-lane streets, with traffic light to moderate (heavy in downtown Courtenay and Comox). There are two significant hills. The roads into Cumberland are almost entirely ascents. Ryan Road peaks at its mid point, with the approach from Courtenay being particularly steep. The

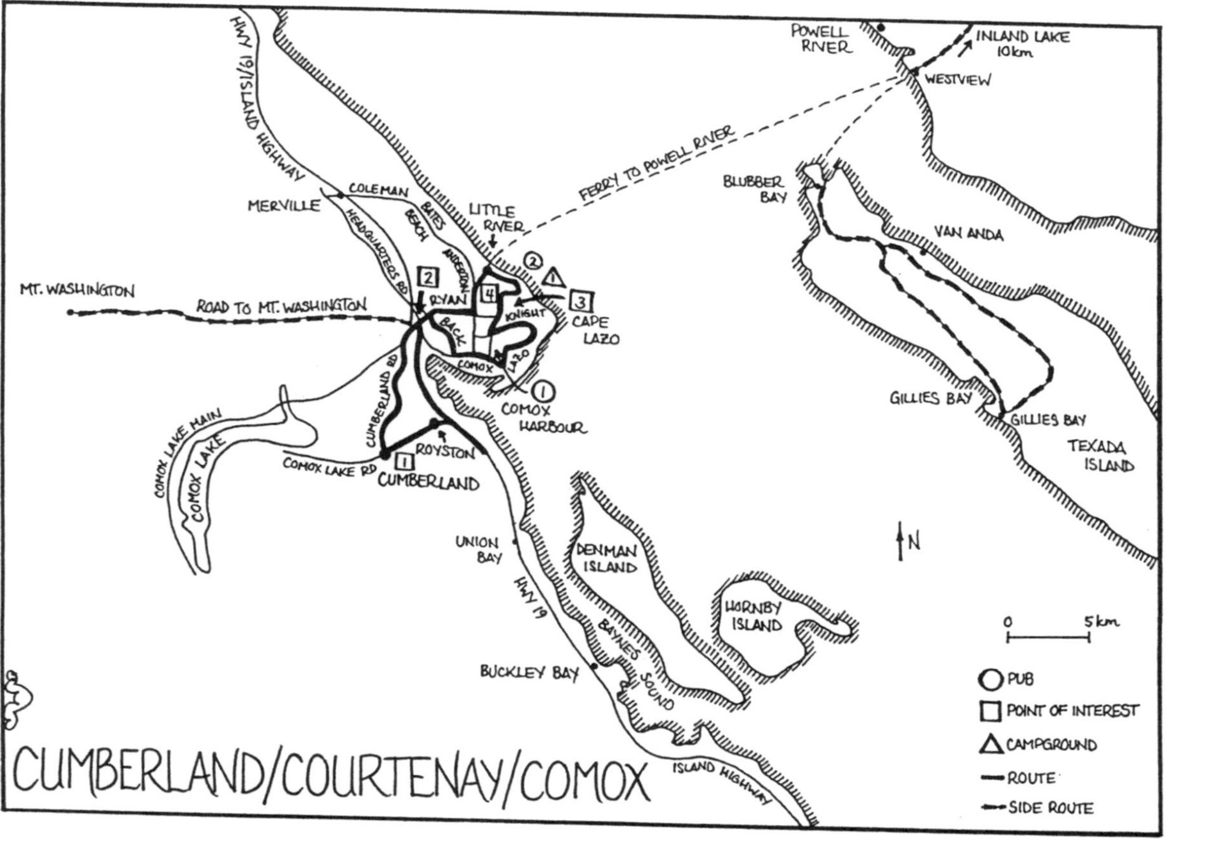
CUMBERLAND/COURTENAY/COMOX
POWELL RIVER
INLAND LAKE 10km
WESTVIEW
FERRY TO POWELL RIVER
BLUBBER BAY
VAN ANDA
GILLIES BAY
GILLIES BAY
TEXADA ISLAND
HWY 19/ISLAND HIGHWAY
MERVILLE
COLEMAN
BATES
BEACH
HEADQUARTERS RD
ANDERTON
LITTLE RIVER
MT. WASHINGTON
ROAD TO MT. WASHINGTON
RYAN
BACK
KNIGHT
COMOX
LAZO
CAPE LAZO
COMOX HARBOUR
CUMBERLAND RD
ROYSTON
CUMBERLAND
COMOX LAKE RD
COMOX LAKE MAIN
COMOX LAKE
UNION BAY
HWY 19
DENMAN ISLAND
HORNBY ISLAND
BAYNES SOUND
BUCKLEY BAY
ISLAND HIGHWAY
N
0
5km
PUB
POINT OF INTEREST
CAMPGROUND
ROUTE
SIDE ROUTE

hill entering Comox on Comox Road can be nerve wracking if the traffic is heavy. The scenic route around Cape Lazo to the Little River ferry terminal is well marked.

There are campgrounds at or near Cumberland, Courtenay and Comox from which to begin and end the route.

Main Route

Road

distance:	60 km; circuit
terrain:	extended flat stretches, two long hills
surface:	paved two-lane, adequate shoulders on the highway; narrow or no shoulders on the backroads
traffic:	light to moderate on the highway; very light on the backroads

Services

bank machines:	Courtenay, Comox, Cumberland, businesses en route
bike repairs:	Courtenay, Comox
liquor store:	Courtenay, Comox, Cumberland
groceries:	Courtenay, Comox, Cumberland
camping:	Kingfisher Oceanside Inn and RV Park, Royston; Kin Beach Campsite, Comox; numerous private sites
hospital:	Comox

My approach

This route can start from campsites at any of the three communities. I usually begin at Royston so I can tackle the extended uphill ride to Cumberland while the day is still cool and my legs fresh. I dally in Cumberland, visit the museum and maybe grab a quick brew at a beer parlour in one of the old hotels on the main street, vestiges of the village's coal mining past.

The backroad into Courtenay, Cumberland Road, is a mostly steady downhill glide into the town centre. The traffic approaching and leaving both the bridges which cross the river toward Comox is always heavy. Comox can be reached via Comox Road along the harbour edge, or along Back Road, which avoids the busy hill into Comox but also lacks the harbour scenery. Downtown Comox has three great pubs within a stone's throw of each other, of which anyone is a desirable stop for lunch. Because I am a history buff, I also linger at the museums in Courtenay and at the Comox Air Force Base.

The Griffin Pub, on the far side of the air force base is well located for a mid-afternoon break, following which I either head back into Courtenay or proceed to Little River before returning.

Cumberland

While today Cumberland is a village, a century ago it was the second-largest population centre on the Island. The Cumberland coal fields were one of the two richest and most accessible on the Pacific coast. The other was Nanaimo. Between 1888 and 1966, when the last mine closed, Cumberland produced twenty-five million tons. Until the discovery of oil in California, Cumberland coal was mainly shipped to San Francisco. Later it was destined for the growing communities of the Island and lower mainland.

Cumberland's population included the second-largest Asian concentration north of San Francisco — mainly Chinese who had come to Canada to escape the deprivations of their homeland, only to be exploited in the mines. Personnel records of the time reveal that virtually no Chinese worked above ground, and Chinese miners were paid at about half the rate of their white co-workers.

I have not stayed at the Cumberland Lakepark Campground just outside town, but its literature refers to fifty sites, washrooms, showers and swimming.

The Cumberland Museum (PI1)

Don't miss the Cumberland Museum. In addition to housing artifacts of Cumberland's Asian and white cultures, the basement has been reconstructed as a mine shaft, complete with sound effects.

Posted in the museum is a list of rules for female teachers dated 1915. It includes:

> "You may not travel beyond the city limits unless you have permission of the chairman of the board."
>
> "You may not dress in bright colours."
>
> "You must wear at least two petticoats."
>
> "You are not to keep company with men."

I can only imagine the effect of running these by either of my twenty-year-old daughters.

The museum also distributes a map of hiking and cycling routes to the old mine sites.

Ginger Goodwin

Cumberland's most famous citizen was a union organizer, for which he was killed. Granted conscientious objector status, Ginger Goodwin was exempted from military service in WW1 but required to work in the mines, an essential industry. Appalled by the conditions in the mines, he set about organizing the workers, anathema to the establishment of the day. His conscientious objector status was retracted, following which he became a draft evader and fugitive. He and some companions hid in the surrounding forest, and were supplied by townspeople until he was discovered by the police and shot, under the guise of resisting arrest.

The policeman was quickly exonnerated, but to the enraged working man Ginger became a martyr of the west coast labour movement, which subsequently influenced unionism across all Canada.

Courtenay

Courtenay, with a population nearing twelve thousand, is the urban and business centre of the Comox Valley. Once a logging and farming centre, it has expanded its focus to include recreation and tourism, and retirement. With the proximity of two popular ski hills, Courtenay is busy year round. It is also a popular retirement destination for air force personnel, having been a favourite posting during their active service.

If heading up-Island, Courtenay is the last large concentration of retail stores on the Island. These are easily accessed in the Driftwood Mall at the south end of town, and in the town centre.

The Courtenay and District Museum (PI2)

Housed in a huge log building, this museum displays artifacts associated with the Valley's logging, aboriginal and early industrial past. During our most recent visit, much of the space was dedicated to a new dinosaur exhibit. In 1988 an extensive deposit of fossils was discovered on the banks of the nearby Puntledge River. Over the next six years these were unearthed and re-assembled to simulate undersea life eighty million years ago, when this area was covered by ocean.

Comox

The Comox Valley is the largest concentration of arable land on Vancouver Island. Now a community of over ten thousand, Comox was originally known as Port Augusta, a sheltered harbour for the ships that serviced the local farms and logging operations.

For the past decade Comox has been highly desirable as an (until recently) affordable residential alternative to Nanaimo and Victoria. Construction there has boomed.

The Lorne Hotel (Pub1)

1770 Comox Road (339-3000)

Of the three pubs in town this is my favourite. It is "reputed to be the oldest licensed British Columbia hotel, in continuous operation since 1879." (Wolferstan) Its owners have maintained the brass and wood decor that captures the charm of visiting an old saloon.

Just down the hill, overlooking Comox's marinas are the Black Fin and Edgewater, two modern pubs worth visiting for their unique construction and views across the harbour. I have puzzled about the market research that would support locating three pubs so close together in a community of this size, but it works well for the visiting cyclist or boater.

Comox Air Force Base (PI3)

The Base is the Valley's largest employer, with 1650 military and civilian employees. Established during WWII to counter the Japanese Pacific threat, it was mothballed at war's end and then re-opened in 1952, as the Cold War began. Squadrons of fighter, search and rescue, and maritime patrol aircraft regularly exercise here. Knight Road parallels a runaway and it is common to witness at close range planes landing and taking off.

The Base houses a museum that is open to the public, and some retired planes are displayed outside.

Hackson Emu Farm (PI4)

Emu farms may soon become a common sight in the Comox Valley. Presently the birds, which can weigh as much as 150 pounds are raised mainly for broodstock, but as their numbers increase they will be processed for food. Emu meat, which is red, is valued for taste, leanness and near absence of cholesterol. Other parts of the bird are also processed. For example, the fat is rendered for ointments used to treat arthritis and sports injuries. And the hides, while difficult to tan, are exceptionally durable.

As soon as we approached the paddock on our first visit to this farm, we were greeted by a committee of these very curious birds, and a large German shepherd dog. The emus pecked at our bikes through the fence, and the dog turned out to be very friendly. He had been confined to the emu paddock as punishment for straying and spent his day playing with these most unusual companions.

The Griffin Pub (Pub2)

Kilmorley and Little River roads (339-4466)

The Griffin occupies a dent of land at the far corner of the air force base. Its walls are festooned with pictures of aircraft in flight, some closeup. The real thing, either taking off or landing, frequently passes overhead.

The pub is owned and managed by Maggie Pickett, her mother and sister. All had previously worked in the hospitality sector and bought the pub in 1991 "for a job." The three women also perform all the maintenance on the premises, making "every day an adventure."

The Griffin has a "Cheers"-like atmosphere and is a second home to service men from the Base and nearby residents. It also has the province's only drive-through off-sales.

Kin Beach Campsite (CG1)

20 sites, swimming

This campground is the best-kept secret on the Island. Created in 1945 by the Kinsmen Club, in 1962 it became a Class C Provincial Park. Class C is a designation reserved for parks which are nominally under the auspices of BC Parks, but administered for primarily local use by a local board. Reference to Kin Beach appears in no guides and there is no signage to assist visitors in finding it. Apparently lacking a formal address, it is located at the south end of Astra Road, just down the hill from the Base (phone 339-5777), and not far from the Griffin Pub.

There is a special area for cyclists, and Kin Beach is never full. In fact it is usually almost empty. The beach, which overlooks the Strait of Georgia, is home to several types of wild flowers which are extinct elsewhere. One occasionally encounters botanists studying them.

This campground is an ideal location from which to conduct this tour, begin the backroads trip up-Island to Campbell River, or reach the Little River ferry terminal — a short, flat ride to the north.

Side Route — Mount Washington

distance:	27 km one way (from Courtenay to base of ski hill); linear
terrain:	extended uphill/downhill
surface:	paved two-lane, mostly without shoulders; last 12 km are gravel surfaced
traffic:	light

This side route comes with a qualifier — I have not yet cycled it. While I was completing this chapter a friend asked if I had included Mount Washington Resort, which recently began transporting cyclists and their bikes to the top of its ski hill (5,280 ft). They can then cycle back down the runs. Cyclists and their bikes are welcome on the chair lift, and the lodge serves food and refreshments in the summer. There is an area to pitch a tent near the Red Chair.

Side Route — Powell River and Texada Island

distance:	various
terrain:	hilly
surface:	paved and gravel two-lane, narrow or no shoulders
traffic:	light

I may be overreaching my mandate by including this side route, which is more appropriately covered in a text on cycling the Sunshine Coast. However, since Alison has set her heart on my securing gainful employment following completion of this book, I will not be writing one on the Sunshine Coast. Moreover, should the camping cyclist opt to remain near the Comox Valley, this route offers some unique diversions.

One reaches Powell River on the ferry from Little River. If it is windy, the ferry ride itself can be an adventure. The waves in this stretch travel from north to south, or vice versa, and the ferry travels east-west. The ferry's hull is soft chined, which is "boaty" talk for rounded. On a windy trip the ferry rolls enough to induce *mal de mer* in even experienced seafarers. Contrary to what I recommend to my friends, a cup of cold bacon fat does not cure this malady.

It was on the ferry trip to Powell River where I first learned that BC Ferries' rider policies are different from those of the Toronto subway. You can't stay on until you feel like disembarking. On the way across Alison and I had participated in a tiff of sufficient magnitude that I elected to remain aboard and return alone to Little River. I discovered that an unattended bicycle which remains after all other passengers and vehicles have disembarked excites the crew, and instigates a search. Finding the bike's owner on the ferry eliminates the only other possibility of his whereabouts — the Strait of Georgia.

Powell River

Powell River is a mill town working hard to re-create itself as a tourist and recreation destination in order to replace mill jobs lost to technology. The community is surrounded by logging roads for which maps are available at the Infocentre. The city of Vancouver can also be reached by a two-day cycle down the Sunshine Coast, which is very hilly, to Langdale and then taking the ferry to Horseshoe Bay.

A unique Powell River attraction is Inland Lake, 15 km to the northeast. This facility, which contains a campground, is completely wheelchair accessible. It includes a flat, crushed-rock path around the edge of the lake, a distance of 12.5 km, and log huts at periodic intervals which include sleeping platforms, a hand waterpump and docks which protrude into the lake to facilitate fishing. Both the town and Inland River can be toured from Little River in a day

Texada Island

Texada is reached from the Powell River ferry dock. If planning to tour Powell River and Texada from a base in the Comox Valley, I recommend camping overnight on Texada. The ferry schedules offer little time for a tour and return trip.

Texada's history reads like a miniature wild west, complete with gold rush, gun fights, saloons and dance halls, and a whiskey still. Its main economic activities are now logging and limestone quarrying, the limestone being shipped in barges to west coast cities for the manufacture of cement.

The roads are free of traffic but hilly. We stayed at the large regional campground at Shelter Point Park (washrooms, showers, swimming) on the shore of Gillies Bay. The manager distributes the Vancouver departure times of the Alaska cruise ships. By applying some rough speed/distance calculations you can have fun estimating when they will pass the mouth of the bay on their way north. This is an impressive sight at night.

We returned by way of Central Road, a logging road accessed by a steep climb from the campground, but mostly level into Sturt Bay. There are grocery stores at Sturt and Gillies bays, and a pub at the former. This particular circuit, which started and ended at the ferry dock, was 28 km.

Comox Valley/Campbell River

The Middle Kingdom

The southern part of this route, Courtenay to the Oyster River, is farmland and country residences. In 1917, near the peak of its operations, the Comox Logging and Railway Company harvested old-growth forest on over 160 km of trackage which crisscrossed the area. Farming followed the timber harvesting and today there is little evidence of the railway.

North of the Oyster River the highway again parallels the shore of the Strait of Georgia, which is much narrower here. Views of varied ocean traffic are common as vessels converge on Discovery Passage, the only inland seaway to the north. Expect to see cargo vessels, ocean-going tugs with barges, pleasure and fish boats, and in the summer the cruise ships which sail between Vancouver and Alaska. You may also encounter an elderly gentleman who for years has cycled this stretch of highway for the excercise several times a week, in all seasons regardless of weather.

This is an easy cycle. The only hill of note is a long steep uphill leaving Courtenay on the Island Highway. The highway itself can be avoided between Merville and Courtenay/Comox by using connecting backroads to its east and west. The traffic is lighter than that experienced south of Courtenay, but still contains a healthy sampling of semi-trailers and RVs.

Campbell River is a bustling community of twenty-seven thousand whose early economy was solely resource based, but has now also evolved into a tourist destination, largely on the strength of being "The Salmon Capital of the World." Elk Falls Provincial Park, on the edge of town, is an ideal location from which to explore the city, surrounding countryside, and nearby Quadra Island.

I do not recommend cycling from Campbell River to Gold River. The

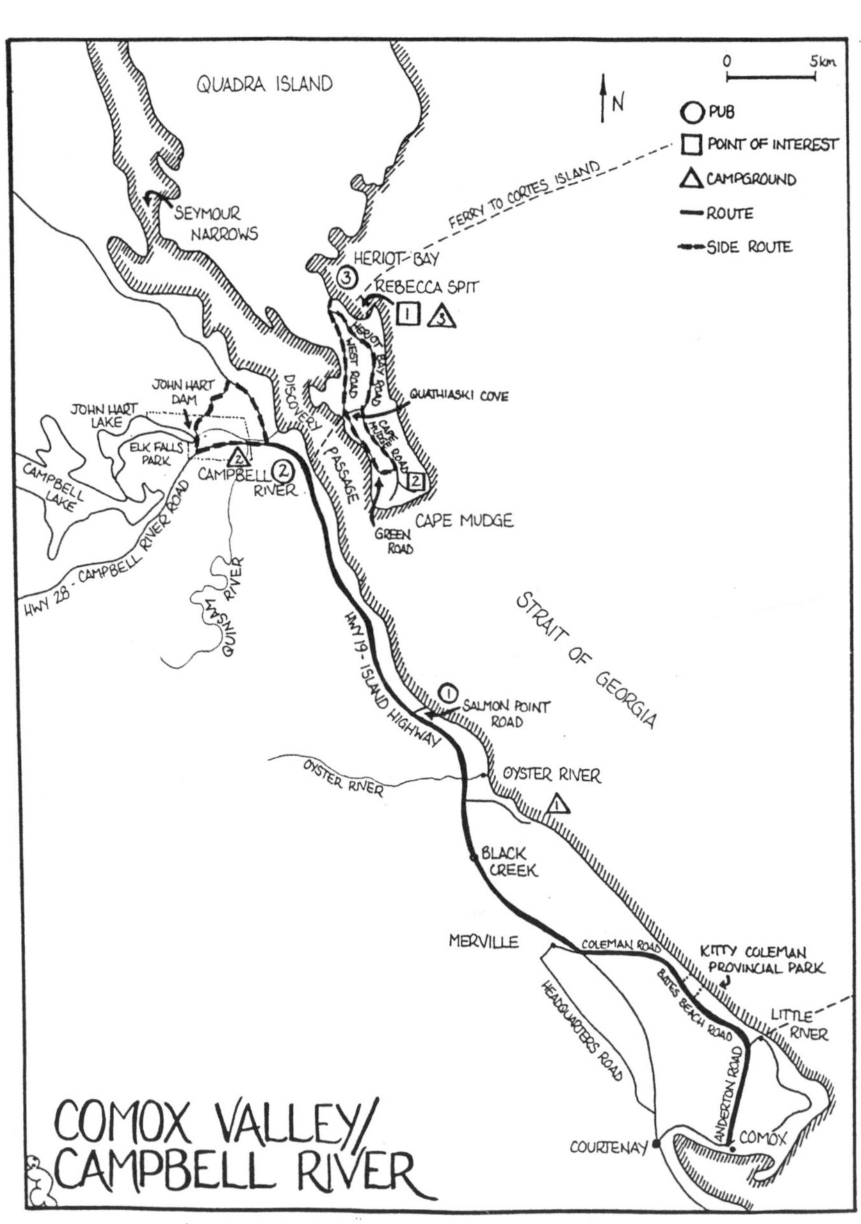
QUADRA ISLAND
0
5km
N
PUB
POINT OF INTEREST
CAMPGROUND
ROUTE
SIDE ROUTE
FERRY TO CORTES ISLAND
SEYMOUR NARROWS
HERIOT BAY
REBECCA SPIT
HERIOT BAY ROAD
WEST ROAD
QUATHIASKI COVE
CAPE MUDGE ROAD
CAPE MUDGE
GREEN ROAD
DISCOVERY PASSAGE
JOHN HART DAM
JOHN HART LAKE
ELK FALLS PARK
CAMPBELL RIVER
CAMPBELL LAKE
HWY 28 - CAMPBELL RIVER ROAD
QUINSAM RIVER
HWY 19 - ISLAND HIGHWAY
STRAIT OF GEORGIA
SALMON POINT ROAD
OYSTER RIVER
OYSTER RIVER
BLACK CREEK
MERVILLE
COLEMAN ROAD
KITTY COLEMAN PROVINCIAL PARK
BATES BEACH ROAD
HEADQUARTERS ROAD
LITTLE RIVER
ANDERTON ROAD
COURTENAY
COMOX
COMOX VALLEY/ CAMPBELL RIVER

road, while scenic, is narrow, full of blind curves and frequented by heavy equipment, including ore trucks from the mine at Buttle Lake. This is one of only two main roads on the Island that I would never dare to cycle.

Main Route

Road

distance:	53 km; linear
terrain:	extended flat stretches, a few gradual hills
surface:	paved two-lane, adequate shoulders on the highway; narrow or no shoulders on the backroads
traffic:	light to moderate on the highway; very light on the backroads

Services

bank machines:	Courtenay, Comox, Campbell River, businesses en route
bike repairs:	Courtenay, Campbell River
liquor store:	Courtenay, Comox, Campbell River, Black Creek (store outlet)
groceries:	Courtenay, Comox, Campbell River, Black Creek, stores en route
camping:	Elk Falls and Miracle Beach provincial parks; various private sites, some ocean front
hospital:	Comox, Campbell River

My approach

When I have cycled this route it has been mainly as a connector between Campbell River and Courtenay/Comox, one leg of an extended trip either up- or down-Island. Whether on the Island Highway or the backroads, it is a pleasant and easy ride. When heading north, The Salmon Point Pub, which overlooks the strait, is well located for a break.

The campground at Elk Falls is a convenient base camp from which to tour the Campbell River downtown and waterfront areas, ascend General Hill to the John Hart Dam, or cross to nearby Quadra Island. You can cycle all three during the extended daylight hours of summer. A more leisurely approach might include camping overnight on Quadra. I recommend fresh legs for ascending General Hill.

The Royal Coachman Pub is a must-see Campbell River landmark.

Miracle Beach Provincial Park (CG1)

193 sites, washrooms, showers, swimming, reservations permitted

Because Miracle Beach is mid-way on this route I seldom stay there, but to first-time visitors I recommend interrupting your journey and camping here, or at least taking a rest break. The park is a destination point in itself and fills quickly in July and August. When full it resembles a well manicured seaside village snuggled in dense trees by the ocean. Facilities include a visitor centre, amphitheater and interpretive programs. The beach rivals Rathtrevor's.

Salmon Point Marine Pub (Pub1)

2176 Salmon Point Road (923-6605)

The turnoff to this pub, which is a couple of kilometres toward the ocean from the highway, is not well marked. The modern but weather-worn wooden building sits on an exposed piece of ocean front next to a man-made boat basin. The property also has a campground which includes seven walk-in campsites.

This is a great location from which to view marine traffic on the Strait of Georgia. On my first visit there, when I was still new to the Island, as I sat eating lunch with a colleague, a tug towing what appeared to be a village passed. Its barge was loaded with cars, trucks, equipment, shelters and residences. Unknown to me at the time, this is a common sight on the coast. A remote coastal camp had been closed and was now being shipped to its next destination.

Campbell River

Campbell River is my favourite Island community. Good times or bad, it exudes an optimism that is immediately apparent to the visitor.

The basis of the Campbell River economy is its abundant resources. The surrounding forests feed pulp and paper and lumber mills and employ over two thousand. The Westmin Mine at the tip of Buttle Lake to the west continues as a successful gold, silver and zinc mine. There is an expanding coal mine just outside town. And until recently Discovery Channel ensured profitable fishing for commercial and sport fishers.

The community has also established itself as a retirement and recreation destination. Retirees seeking a modern lifestyle and reasonably priced homes are still only a hundred-kilometre drive from the ferry to Vancouver. Tourists are attracted by the recreation alternatives of the surrounding lakes and mountains, and the nearly year-round salmon fishing. The prestigious Tyee Club was founded in 1924. Membership is open to anyone who has caught a salmon weighing over 13.6 kg (30 lbs) on light tackle from an open rowboat.

The city is easy to tour by bike, since most of its sights are accessed from the main highway which doubles as the main street of town. Of particular interest are government wharves, the museum, the Discovery Pier (from which rods can be rented and salmon caught), and the Tyee Spit. The Tyee Spit is a float-plane terminal and the sole connection to civilization for many coastal logging and fishing camps.

The Royal Coachman Neighbourhood Pub (Pub2)

84 Dogwood Street (286-0231)

The Royal Coachman is one of the more imposing and unique buildings of any sort on the Island. It was designed by an English architect now living in Campbell River and styled after the tudor buildings of his native York. Constructed using time-honoured European methods, its timbers are seasoned old-growth fir and yellow cedar, salvaged from logging bridges in areas where harvesting operations have ended.

The pub derives its name from the winning entry in a contest to name it. It was reportedly the favourite trout fly of Roderick Haig-Brown, world-renowned Campbell River angler, magistrate, conservationist and philosopher.

Ken Phillips, owner and founder, takes special pride in his pub's menu which is prepared by two of the region's top chefs.

Elk Falls Provincial Park (CG2)

121 sites, swimming

Elk Falls straddles the Campbell and Quinsam rivers and Highway 28, the road to Gold River. The best campsites are those on the banks of the Quinsam. Unfortunately these sites fillup quickly, and because they are near a children's play area can be noisy.

The park contains an extensive network of hiking trails, a falls and a fish hatchery. The map showing a swimming hole three kilometres or so to the west can be misleading to the first-time cyclist to the area. This is the infamous General Hill. Even if you didn't need a swim when you started for the swimming hole, you will when you get there.

As indicated earlier this campground is an ideal location from which to explore the surrounding area. If you feel like a cold beer and a little adventure, try the Quinsam Hotel just along the road in nearby Campbellton. I once stopped in, asked for mug of beer and was told it only came in glasses. If they served mugs the clientele would steal them. This is not a watering hole for the faint of heart wearing lycra cycling pants.

Side Route — John Hart Dam

distance:	27 km; circuit
terrain:	uphill/downhill
surface:	paved two-lane, mostly without shoulders
traffic:	light

While the subject of this route is the dam, it is unlikely to be the first-time cyclist's main recollection of it. More likely, that will be General Hill, an ascent of 240 m in a distance of 3 km. The dam, created to generate hydro-electric power, is accessed by a turnoff near the top of the hill. There is an excellent view along John Hart Lake from here, provided your blood pressure has dropped back sufficiently for your vision to recover!

The return to town can be straight back down the hill (check brakes first), or via a series of backroads that connects to the Island Highway near Duncan Bay, about seven kilometres north of Campbell River. The Ministry of Forests map, Campbell River Forest District, details this route as well as the locations of a series of primitive campsites further inland on the shores of Campbell Lake.

Side Route — Quadra Island

distance:	25 km; circuit
terrain:	hilly
surface:	paved two-lane, narrow or no shoulders
traffic:	light

The ferry to Quadra Island departs from downtown Campbell River on a near-hourly basis during the day. On the ten-minute crossing to Quathiaski Cove passengers will usually experience the currents in Discovery Passage, which attain seven knots and more, and make this stretch of water such a desirable feeding ground for salmon. During past salmon runs I have witnessed scores of small boats fishing at the south end of Discovery Passage.

Cape Mudge, at the island's southern tip, is "one of the most notoriously vicious areas in the Strait of Georgia" (Wolferstan). A combination of strong southeast winds and a tide from the north creates tumultuous seas that have wrecked vessels as they attempted to enter Discovery Passage.

Quadra is an island that could easily be a cycling holiday destination in itself. My familiarity with Quadra is limited to a few of its most notable landmarks. We have yet to explore much of the network of paved and logging roads which crisscross the island, or other landmarks like Cape Mudge with its lighthouse and petroglyphs.

Heriot Bay Inn (Pub3)

The village of Heriot Bay contains docks, businesses and stores (including grocery and liquor), and the Heriot Bay Inn, an intimate pub which holds some fond memories for me, none of which relate to cycling. In 1982, on a family sailing trip to nearby Desolation Sound the casing for my engine's impellor broke and we had to berth at the Inn's dock and await a part to be flown to us. During these two days some of our time was spent in the pub where I viewed for the first time television programming received by satellite transmission, and Australian Rules Rugby. If that wasn't enough excitement, we could also watch the Cortes Island ferry arrive and depart from its nearby wharf.

Shortly after, unable to cope with the emotional strain of sailing, I became a cyclist.

Rebecca Spit Provincial Park (PI1, CG3)

camping at adjoining First Nations campground; swimming, washrooms, showers

Quadra Island was a strategic location on the border between the Kwagiulth and Coast Salish tribes, and therefore the objective of ancient battles. Rebecca Spit is believed to have been the site of a complex of Coast Salish fortifications, as evidenced by a network of trenches in the park which are thought to be two hundred to four hundred years old.

There is no camping permitted in the park, but the local First Nations band has established a beachfront campground at the end of the bay, adjoining the spit. This is an excellent location from which to explore the rest of the island.

Kwagiulth First Nations Museum (PI2)

Located in the First Nations village of Cape Mudge, this museum is the other home of repatriated potlatch articles, the history of which has been detailed in "Sointula/Alert Bay, A Tale of Two Cultures."

Campbell River/Sayward/Woss Camp

"Do not let your love of the wilderness blind you to the needs of your fellow man."
(from a poster in a North Island restaurant)

This route has two personalities, with Sayward the dividing point. I consider the stretch between Campbell River and Sayward to be a buffer between the central Island, with its denser population and more diverse economy, and the North Island, sparsely populated and where logging is king. Heading north on this stretch, human activity is gradually reduced to two categories, logging and outdoor recreation. This theme continues between Sayward and Woss Camp and beyond, almost to Port McNeill.

The Nimpkish Valley is a paradise for the outdoors enthusiast. An extensive network of logging roads and wilderness campgounds, by-products of logging, open the forests for fishing, hunting, hiking and cycling. Detailed maps are available at Infocentres and from the forest companies, and I recommend them. This is also the last region of railway logging in the province, and rail overpasses frequently cross the highway.

Except for logging roads, the Island Highway is the only route through this area. North of Campbell River the highway moves inland across mountains, a ribbon of asphalt through wilderness. A few kilometres outside Campbell River the traffic becomes light to very light, even in the summer months. The highway is mostly two-lane with narrow or no shoulders. The terrain comprises long hills, some of which are steep, and extended flat stretches. There are expansive views of mountains and vast forests. Bear, deer and elk sightings are common.

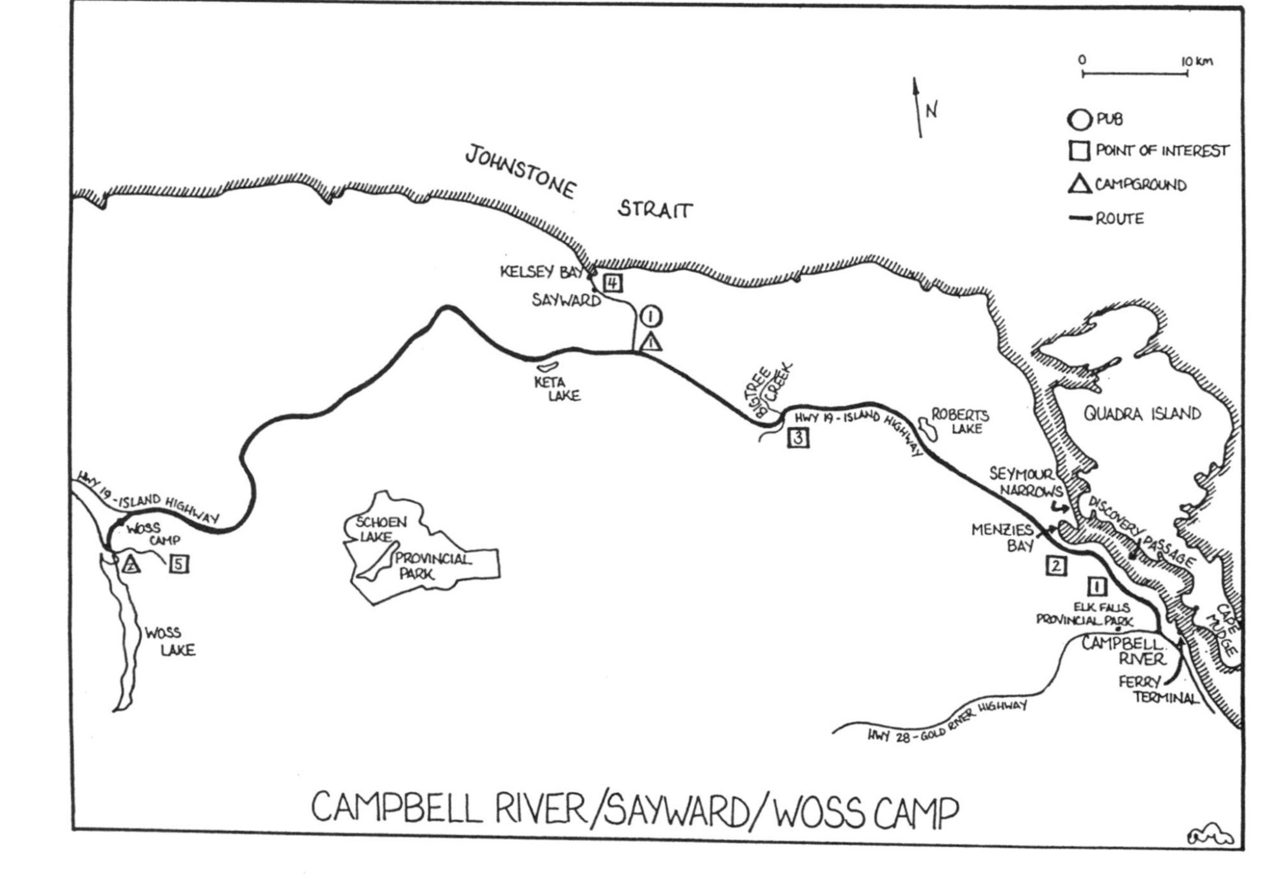
0
10 km
N
PUB
POINT OF INTEREST
CAMPGROUND
ROUTE
JOHNSTONE STRAIT
KELSEY BAY
SAYWARD
4
1
KETA LAKE
BIGTREE CREEK
HWY 19 - ISLAND HIGHWAY
3
ROBERTS LAKE
QUADRA ISLAND
SEYMOUR NARROWS
DISCOVERY PASSAGE
MENZIES BAY
2
1
ELK FALLS PROVINCIAL PARK
CAPE MUDGE
CAMPBELL RIVER
FERRY TERMINAL
HWY 28 - GOLD RIVER HIGHWAY
HWY 19 - ISLAND HIGHWAY
WOSS CAMP
5
SCHOEN LAKE PROVINCIAL PARK
WOSS LAKE
CAMPBELL RIVER/SAYWARD/WOSS CAMP

In the summer this route can be hot. The heat combined with the long hills quickly induce dehydration. The only mid-route services, including drinking water, are stores at Roberts Lake and Sayward. There are rest areas at fifty-kilometre intervals which contain picnic tables, toilets, and shade trees, but no drinking water. However, rest areas are a source of recreational vehicles from which to beg water. I carry two litres with me, but on a recent trip I needed ten.

There are dozens of roadside streams providing an excellent source of cool drinking water provided it can be purified. The first chance I had after completing this stretch, I bought my purifier.

In the spring and summer there are no-see-ums and black flies, both objectionable little biters. When travelling this part of the Island I keep my repellant handy.

Main Route

Road

distance:	135 km; linear
terrain:	long hills, some steep, and exended flat stretches
surface:	paved two-lane, narrow or no shoulders
traffic:	moderate near Campbell River; remainder light to very light

Services

bank machines:	Campbell River, some stores and bars give debit card advances
bike repairs:	Campbell River
liquor store:	Campbell River, Sayward (store), Woss Camp (store)
groceries:	Campbell River, Sayward, Woss Camp, Roberts Lake (limited)
camping:	numerous private, provincial and forestry sites
hospital:	Campbell River

My approach

The route, although long and hilly, can be accomplished in a single day. However, depending on level of fitness and body type, fatigue and dehydration may be factors. As indicated earlier there are no services between Sayward and Woss, including no sources of safe drinking water.

Both times that I have cycled this route I have been heading north and have taken two days. The first time, in 1981 we had never been to the

North Island, and stopped at Sayward thinking we would sightsee. The second time in 1995 I was travelling alone and knew by then that there were no sights in Sayward to justify stopping. I also knew that there was one incredible hill immediately north and that I was already tired from the heat.

Fisherboy Campground, just off the highway on the turnoff to Sayward, is my favourite private campground on the Island. Its location is ideal from which to explore Sayward and Kelsey Bay, two adjoining communities closer to the coast, and be positioned to hit the road the next morning. For some, Sayward and Kelsy Bay may represent the first time to view a community that still derives its existence almost exclusively from the woods.

Elk Falls Pulp and Paper Mill (PI1)

This huge mill is the largest single employer in the area. While it no longer dominates the local economy as it once did, the sight of smoke and steam rising from its stacks still signifies prosperity — the world markets for its products are healthy, as are labour relations within the plant.

Two years ago on a sunny day in early autumn, while touring Campbell River with a colleague, we experienced thick, smelly mill smog in downtown. I asked the local Economic Development Officer whether this had a detrimental effect on business. His response, "No, it's the smell of money."

Seymour Narrows Lookout (PI2)

This rest area overlooks Ripple Rock, which in 1958 was the site of the world's largest non-nuclear explosion. This huge twin-peaked hazard had claimed numerous ships and lives since first being discovered in 1792. Tunnels were drilled into each peak and filled with explosives. The ensuing explosion shattered windows in Campbell River, eight kilometres to the south.

Because of the treacherous currents and huge whirlpools, Seymour Narrows is still considered one of the most dangerous hazards to navigation on the BC coast.

Big Tree Creek Fish Hatchery (PI3)

This hatchery raises stock for commercial fish farms. Select mature adult salmon are removed from their pens and "milked" for their eggs and semen, which are then commingled to fertilize the eggs. After they have hatched, the thousands of tiny fish are kept in open-air tanks, where they are fed and tested and treated for disease. When they reach a desired size they are trucked to pens where they will complete their lives before being harvested.

Fisherboy Campground (CG1)

20 sites, washrooms, showers

The tent sites at Fisherboy are around the edge of a huge meadow, surrounded by trees. The campground is immaculately maintained and always quiet. Its location near the main highway facilitates making camp and then proceeding into Sayward or the pub, which is five kilometres toward Sayward.

During my last stay there I acquired an indication of the volume of tourism we derive from Europe. Virtually every motorhome was a rental driven by a visitor from Germany or France. The owner of Fisherboy told me that these visitors now comprise a significant percentage of his clientele.

Sayward/Kelsey Bay(PI4)

Sayward, a community of twelve hundred, exists for logging. It is home to those who log the surrounding forests, and harvested logs are trucked to adjoining Kelsey Bay for sorting and booming. Before the highway to Port Hardy was completed, a ferry which connected that community to the rest of the Island docked here. The remnants of the wharf remain.

A few years ago Sayward was flooded during fall rains, partly the result of years of logging on the surrounding mountains.

There is evidence that Sayward is becoming a retirement destination for those attracted by affordable property and a semi-isolated lifestyle.

Coral Reef (Pub1)

Sayward Road (282-3648)

The first time I passed the Coral Reef it had just been constructed and I could have been excused for assuming it was just a residence. In fact it is a slightly modified standard house design; the tables are in what were meant to be the living and dining rooms.

The pub is owned by Art and Nan Pampu, commercial fishers who recognized “the signs of changing times” and decided to seek an alternate livelihood. It is a drop-in for local loggers and an opportunity for the casual eavesdropper to acquire some logging jargon. The Pampus have also set up a display table for distributing maps and brochures supplied by the logging companies.

A perspective on North Island logging

Like most Islanders I am reasonably familiar with the environmental issues surrounding logging. It is impossible to live here and not be. My research for this book assisted in my understanding of the magnitude of logging, particular on the North Island. The cyclist travelling from Campbell River to Woss, and then on to Port McNeill passes through the tree farm licences first of MacMillan Bloedel and then Canfor. Both companies encourage visits to their offices, distribute information on their operations in the area and conduct tours. Regardless of your position on logging issues, these are bound to expand your understanding of this industry. Below are some statistics, extracted from information which these companies make available to the public, that illustrate the immensity of their North Island operations.

MacMillan Bloedel Limited (Menzies Bay, Kelsey Bay, and Eve River divisions)

- manages 280,000 hectares of North Island forests (nearly 9 percent of the total land mass of Vancouver Island)
- this represents 128.2 million cubic meters of some of the finest softwood (conifers, mainly balsam, hemlock and western red cedar) in the world
- 2.2 million cubic meters harvested annually
- 47 million seedlings planted in North Island forests

Canadian Forest Products Ltd. (Nimpkish Valley, Englewood Division)

- covers a length of 96 km, the equivalent of 20 percent of the Island's total length
- supports jobs for four hundred local employees and 150 contractors
- annual operating expenses total $65 million
- operates and maintains 1220 km of logging roads and 90 km of railroad track
- logs and plants 1.5 million trees annually

Woss Camp (PI5)

Woss, population six hundred, is the centre for Canfor's Nimkish Valley operations. It contains the Englewood Logging Division's main office and shops. This division maintains the Island's last remaining logging railway, which comprises four diesel electric locomotives and five hundred pieces of rolling stock. The equipment and track are continuously upgraded. In the Nimkish Valley it is still cost effective to transfer the logging trucks' loads to trains, and then haul them to the company's sorting and booming grounds at Beaver Cove.

Woss is also the home of Number 113, a restored 1920 steam locomotive that in the summer is paired with a restored coach to carry tourists through some of Canfor's Nimpkish Valley operations.

Woss Lake Campground (CG2)

24 sites, swimming

This wilderness campground, maintained by Canfor, is reached by cycling about three kilometres of well-marked logging road from Woss Camp. It is a beautiful spot, close to an alpine lake with a sandy beach, protected by trees, and free. However my feelings toward it are ambivalent. On the two occasions I have camped there I have arrived hot and tired, and perhaps even a little cranky, and this is the noisiest campground I have ever encountered.

During my most recent visit to the Woss Lake Campground I met a retired French engineer named Rolph. Every year Rolph flies with his bike to a different part of the world and tours for a month. This year he had started at Edmonton, crossed the BC Interior to Prince Rupert, and was now cycling from Port Hardy to Vancouver. It was his first trip to Canada. Over a cold beer at my picnic table we shared recollections of our trips thus far. And I tried to convince him that Canada was more than a few towns separated by hundreds of kilometres of mountains. We ate breakfast together next morning at the restaurant beside the highway, following which we would go our separate ways.

When we had finished our last cup of coffee, Rolph looked across the table at me and said "Well we might as well get going. It's not like we have anything else to do. And it sure beats working." That comment has remained with me during the writing of this book. It symbolizes my wonderful summer of 1995.

Sointula/Alert Bay

A Tale of Two Cultures

Cormorant and Malcolm islands are connected to Port McNeill by short ferry rides. I have only visited them once, on an impulse while researching this book. I had stopped at McNeill on the way to Hardy and was waiting for Alison to arrive by car. Alison, who is far more curious about out-of-the-way places than I, first suggested we go there. I now wish we'd made the trip years before.

Cormorant Island is almost entirely covered by the village of Alert Bay, which can be toured by Fir Street along the edge of the bay. On disembarking from the ferry, the area of town to the left is the Whe-La-La-U Reserve, to the right the white community. Non-aboriginals are welcome on the reserve, as are aboriginals in the white community. I have difficulty defining the vibrancy of Alert Bay without appearing to emulate a tourism brochure — which is this incompetent writer's cop-out for "It's a different world. You are best to sample it for yourself." The Infocentre distributes a free walking tour guide, which identifies the locations of points of interest and provides backgrounds.

Malcolm Island is a former Finnish commune, with a unique history. Serene and tidy, it is an easy cycle for anyone seeking a break from long days of touring. While its fascinating history is much in evidence, the highlight for us was our stay at Bere Point.

Traffic is busy on Fir Street in Alert Bay, but inconsequential because it moves very slowly. It is light on Malcolm Island. The roads are two-lane and paved except for the route to Bere point, which is mostly logging road. The only hill of note on either section of the route leads to Oceanview Campsite in Alert Bay.

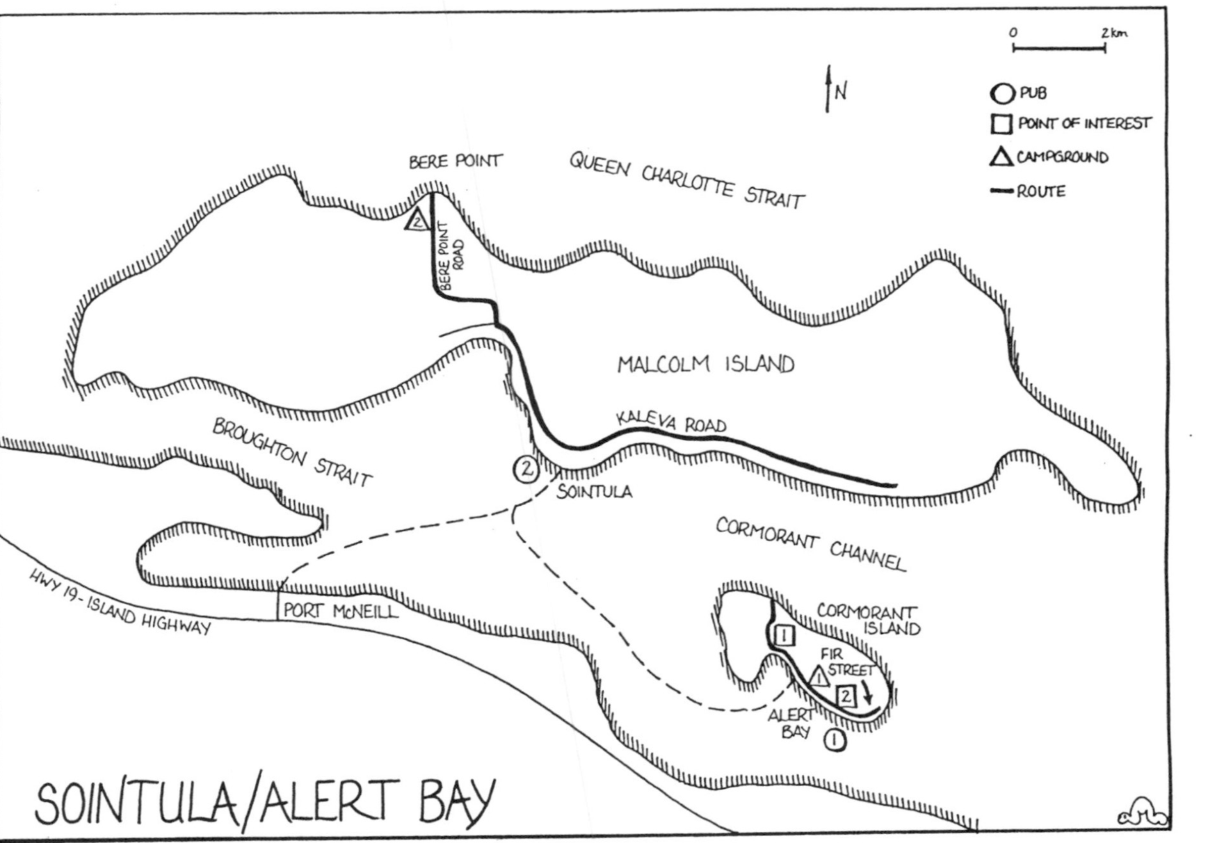

0
2km
N
PUB
POINT OF INTEREST
CAMPGROUND
ROUTE
BERE POINT
QUEEN CHARLOTTE STRAIT
BERE POINT ROAD
MALCOLM ISLAND
KALEVA ROAD
BROUGHTON STRAIT
SOINTULA
CORMORANT CHANNEL
CORMORANT ISLAND
FIR STREET
ALERT BAY
PORT McNEILL
HWY 19 - ISLAND HIGHWAY
SOINTULA/ALERT BAY

Main Route

Road

distance:	30 km; circuit
terrain:	long flat stretches; short hills; steep hill to Oceanview Campsite, Alert Bay
surface:	paved two-lane, narrow or no shoulders; logging road to Bere Point
traffic:	moderate to heavy in Alert Bay, very light on Malcolm Island

Services

bank machines:	Port McNeill, Alert Bay, Sointula
bike repairs:	Campbell River, Port Hardy
liquor store:	Port McNeill, Alert Bay, Sointula (co-op)
groceries:	Port McNeill, Alert Bay, Sointula
camping:	Oceanview Campsite, Bere Point, private sites on Malcolm Island
hospital:	Port McNeill, Alert Bay

My approach

This is a short trip and can be done in a single day from Port McNeill, but I recommend at least one overnight stay on either island. There is much to see and absorb on both islands. A fresh roll of film is a must.

We went first to Alert Bay, toured both sides of the community, mostly along Fir Street, and stayed overnight at the Oceanview Campsite. The second day we ferried to Sointula, toured the village and some of the east end of the island, and then camped at Bere Point. Next time we will go straight to Bere Point, set up camp, and then tour Alert Bay as a day trip.

Alert Bay

Before the North Island was accessible by road, Alert Bay was a transportation hub. It was a sheltered stop-off for fishing and passenger boats. During the era when logging and fishing dominated the economy, Alert Bay was a very wealthy community. It is presently emerging as a popular destination for tourists and boaters who find Desolation Sound to the south too crowded.

During our visit we were curious about the large number of taxis in this small village (population 700). These are the vestige of a much larger fleet from the days when the town had money.

U'mista Cultural Centre (PI1)

Located on the Reserve, this site is one of two (the other is on Quadra Island) museums built to showcase repatriated potlatch artifacts. Potlatches were central to Nimpkish culture. They were held to celebrate important events like births, deaths and marriages. During the ceremony the guests received gifts, usually ceremonial coppers, masks and rattles — all highly valued by the tribe. The more gifts distributed, the higher the status of the giver.

The wisdom of the time, primarily as defined by the Anglican Church, held that potlatches impeded attempts to "civilize" the native population. The federal government was pressured into enacting legislation prohibiting potlatches. The ceremonies continued underground and in 1921, forty-five people were charged with participating in a potlatch. Individuals were offered leniency if their individual tribes agreed to surrender all their potlatch artifacts. These confiscated items were distributed to museums in Ottawa, Toronto, and to private collectors.

Those who had lost their treasures, which represented the soul of the Nimpkish people, never forgot their loss. After years of effort, the artifacts are now being gradually returned and are on display at the centre. U'mista also serves as an education centre, teaching young people their traditional language and ceremonies.

U'mista is more than a museum, it represents the revitalization of a culture.

Oceanview Campsite (CG1)

20 sites, washrooms, showers

In the brochures Oceanview is described as overlooking Mitchell Bay. It does, from a height of fifty meters. I advise planning a sightseeing schedule which minimizes the frequency of pedaling up this hill. During our stay our only fellow camper was a young Japanese man. We first noticed him hiking past us under a huge backpack. Some time later he returned with another. It transpired that he was a kayaker and had paddled from Robson Bight. The packs were his gear and collapsible boat. In addition to being high, this campground is also two kilometres from shore.

Adjoining the campground is Gator Gardens, a natural swamp fed by an underground spring. The village has laid a network of boardwalk trails through it to assist hikers.

Nimpkish Burial Grounds (PI2)

The burial grounds contain the century-old totem poles of deceased members of the Nimpkish band. We asked why this cemetery was not on the

Reserve side of the village. Before colonization, Cormorant Island was used by the Natives only as a burial ground. They began to reside here permanently at the end of the last century, attracted by jobs at the newly built saltery. When the Reserve was established, it was at the other side of the bay.

The burial grounds are sacred, and although open, unauthorized entry is considered a sacrilege. While photographing the totem poles Alison inadvertently set foot inside and was loudly reprimanded by the driver of a passing car.

Nimpkish Hotel and Pub (Pub1)

The Nimpkish Hotel was originally located on the other side of the bay. In 1920 its owners applied for a liquor license and were denied because the hotel was on the Reserve. Undaunted, the owners barged it across to the white community's shore. Toward the end of this exercise the barge washed ashore, where it sits today. The present owner, Imelda Klotz, led us down to the beach from where we could see the barge still resting under the hotel. Later, back in Port McNeill we were told the floor of the pub is threatened with flooding at very high tides. I haven't been able to verify this, but what an idea for a party!

When we arrived the pub had been recently renovated, and a small outside patio constructed on the beach.

Imelda was kind enough to offer us a beer, so we settled in to people-watch. Behind us were two men playing chess. As it happens, chess enjoys a near cult following in Alert Bay and neighbouring Sointula. All the bars stock chess sets, and players routinely challenge each other. There is even an informal chess hierarchy supported by "ladder" play.

Malcolm Island

At the turn of the century, Finnish pioneers attempted to establish a co-operative colony on the Island. Sointula, the island's only village, means "harmony." Members initially derived their livelihoods from fishing, and later farming and logging. The dream failed and after a series of disasters, including a fire in the community's meeting hall, half the members left the island in 1905. While visiting we learned that another of the "disasters" was the expectation by some that members share their wives and daughters.

The island's economic bases are fishing, and to a lesser extent, logging. The commercial fleet which docks at the north end of Sointula supplies two local processors. Malcolm Islanders seek to preserve the island's unique ambience, and particularly welcome low impact tourists like hikers and cyclists. Visitors can purchase a detailed map of the island at the gallery at the top of the ferry dock. This map also includes the logging roads, which we did not travel but were told are in good condition and have some great ocean views.

A visit to the cemetary at the south end of Sointula confirms Malcolm Island's Finnish heritage.

Bilge Pub (Pub2)

Malcolm Island Inn (973-6555)

The Bilge Pub is a quiet pub near the ferry terminal in the basement of the Malcolm Island Inn. There is a view across the water from some of the tables. This pub has no off-sales. It operates under a lounge license which does not permit them, as we found out on a Sunday, when the co-op liquor outlet was also closed.

Our memories from here are of halibut cheeks — a seldom available and expensive west coast delicacy. Alison overheard a gentleman who we later learned was named Bob Davis mention to his buddies that he had some halibut cheeks, and commented that she loved them. When we were leaving one of the buddies suggested we wait, that Bob had gone to his room for halibut cheeks. He returned with these and some smoked salmon, for which he charged next to nothing. Why he kept them in his room is a mystery. A lot of people I know do not keep halibut cheeks in their rooms.

We shared them that night with our friends at the campsite, who contributed hamburger helper. This lent a brand new meaning to "surf and turf."

Bere Point Regional Park (CG2)

about 8 sites, beach, picnic shelter

When friends ask for highlights of my summer spent cycling to research my book, Bere Point is always near the top. The park itself is primitive — hard ground and a couple of outhouses. But all sites are private, being surrounded by trees and bushes, and each faces the beach.

We learned about this little-known campground during a chance encounter on the island with an acquaintance from Nanaimo. He was camped there with his family partly for the chance to view whales. Bere Point is a pebble spit, and whales sometimes use it for rubbing.

Alison and I finished making camp late in the afternoon, and decided to walk along the spit before supper. We were lucky enough to see a grey whale only a few meters from shore. The next morning at breakfast we were also treated to a pod of killer whales circling in front of our campsite.

Telegraph Cove/ Port McNeill/Port Hardy

"The king is dead! Long live the king!"

South and central Vancouver Islanders seldom venture north to ports McNeill and Hardy. Not that this involves extended travel by the standards of many Canadians, particularly those on the prairies. It's just that there is so much to occupy us closer to home. When I cycled there in 1995 I was unsure what to expect. I had visited for the first time on a bicycle fourteen years previously, and had made only a few quick business trips over recent years. During this period these communities, both heavily resource based, seemed to be dogged by controversy and bad luck. Specifically:

- the huge open-pit copper mine outside Port Hardy, which at peak operation employed hundreds, was being phased-out of operation.
- economists and environmentalists had influenced forest management legislation which curtailed forest harvesting, and jeopardized hundreds of jobs.
- the decline of the salmon fishery threatened the North Island's commercial fleet.

The bright spots are outdoor recreation and tourism. Other Canadians, Americans and Europeans are discovering the North Island in droves.

What I learned in the summer of 1995 intrigued me. The village of Telegraph Cove literally overflows with sport fishermen and whale watchers. Port McNeill continues to cling obstinately to its logging past. And a

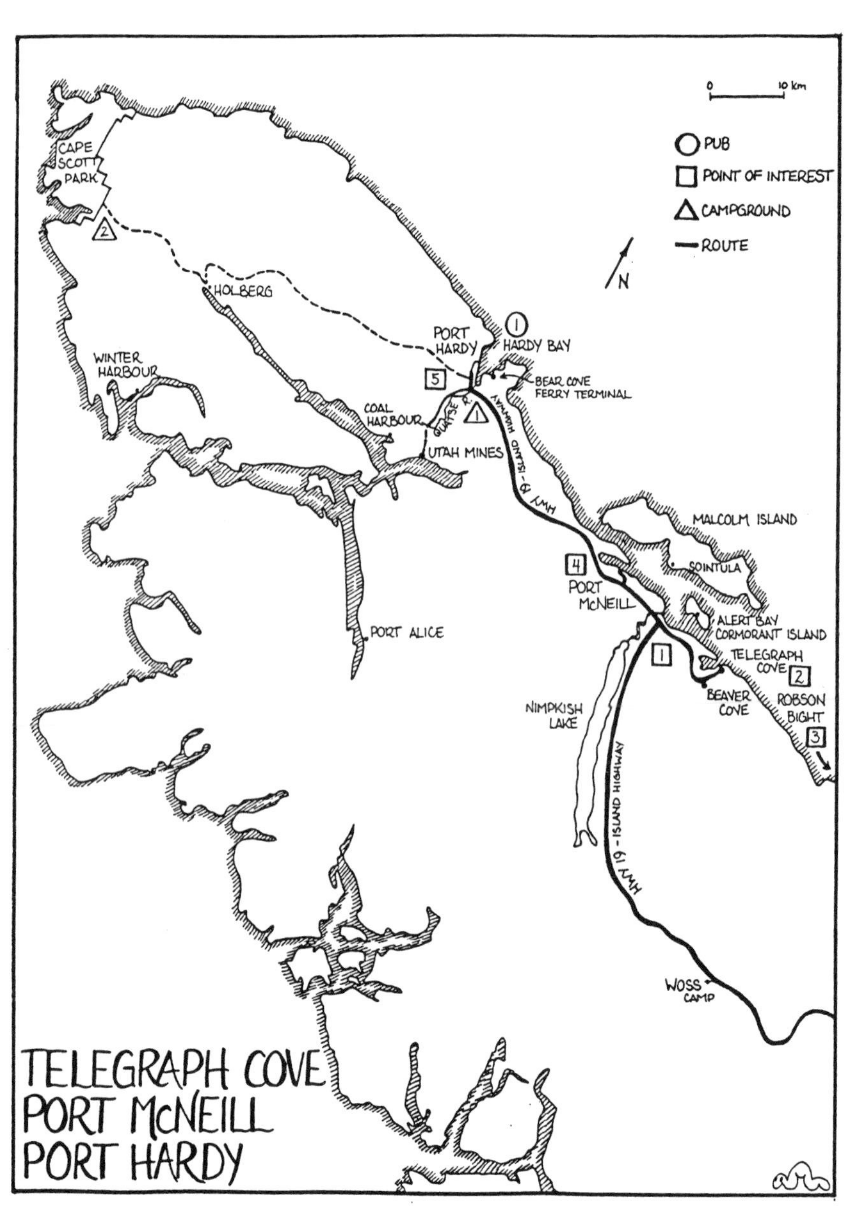

0
10 km
PUB
POINT OF INTEREST
CAMPGROUND
ROUTE
N
CAPE SCOTT PARK
2
HOLBERG
PORT HARDY
1
HARDY BAY
BEAR COVE FERRY TERMINAL
WINTER HARBOUR
5
COAL HARBOUR
QUATSE R.
1
UTAH MINES
HWY 19 - ISLAND HIGHWAY
MALCOLM ISLAND
SOINTULA
4
PORT McNEILL
ALERT BAY
CORMORANT ISLAND
1
TELEGRAPH COVE
2
BEAVER COVE
ROBSON BIGHT
3
PORT ALICE
NIMPKISH LAKE
HWY 19 - ISLAND HIGHWAY
WOSS CAMP
TELEGRAPH COVE
PORT McNEILL
PORT HARDY

surprisingly vibrant Port Hardy is busy re-defining itself as a tourist destination.

The route between Woss and Port NcNeill is an extension of Sayward/ Woss, without the extreme hills. The only services en route are available from a small store at Nimpkish Camp. As with the previous route, pack extra water or a purifier. While I didn't experience it myself, I'm told that on sunny days by late morning the wind blows hard from north to south along Nimpkish Lake, a wind surfer's utopia. It can be a significant help or hindrance to the cyclist, depending on direction of travel.

The hill from Port McNeill back up to the highway is challenging. The road between Port McNeill and Port Hardy is downright boring, except for one rest area with an expansive view of Broughton Strait. Expect nondescript, narrow-shouldered black top, rolling hills, long flat stretches and stunted trees. Don't be surprised if the weather changes toward Hardy. The extreme North Island is often affected by fronts from Queen Charlotte Strait and the open Pacific that don't reach much further south. On both my cycling trips it rained during this stretch, after having been sunny until Port McNeill.

I learned the hard way that in spite of the many campgrounds in Port Hardy, in the summer there is a desperate shortage of sites on days when the ferry from Prince Rupert arrives. Passengers disembark late in the day after being cooped-up for hours and elect to camp immediately, rather than begin the long trip down-Island. I recommend reserving ahead.

Finally, this is not traditional pub country. With one exception the watering holes are bars and beer halls attached to hotels.

Main Route

Road

distance:	58 km; linear
terrain:	rolling hills, some long; extended flat streches
surface:	paved two-lane, narrow or no shoulders
traffic:	light

Services

bank machines:	Port McNeill, Port Hardy
bike repairs:	Port McNeill, Port Hardy
liquor store:	Port McNeill, Port Hardy
groceries:	Port McNeill, Port Hardy
camping:	various private and forestry sites
hospital:	Port McNeill, Port Hardy

My approach

I have covered this route twice, both times one-way from south to north. I met other cyclists travelling in the opposite direction also one-way, having arrived in Port Hardy by ferry. The route can be accomplished in a day, but not with comfort if a visit is planned to Telegraph Cove, where there is a huge private campground (which is often full). Another option, particularly if also planning to spend time on Cormorant and Malcolm islands, is to visit Telegraph Cove first, and then proceed to Port McNeill. It has a campground near the ferry terminal.

My campground of choice is the Quatse River Campground, in the regional park just outside Port Hardy. It offers quiet, privacy and proximity to town.

Cyclists seldom travel the route both ways, possibly because it is so distant from their homes that shortage of time necessitates a faster return medium. In my case, this has been the bus back to Nanaimo.

Bicycles on buses

To the bus companies, hauling a bicycle is simple. The bike, enclosed in a container to protect the luggage of other passengers, is tossed in the cargo bay and returned to the rider on arrival at destination. The rider's role is to locate a container for the bike. In the past for me this has been a simple and amusing process. If the local bike store did not have a bicycle-sized used cardboard box lying around, then a furniture store would have an old mattress box. For years I have counseled fellow travellers on the effectiveness of this technique, which also enhances communication skills, specifically those associated with begging.

On my last trip I was confronted with the obsolescence of my own advice. The bicycle store no longer retains its old packing boxes. They are now valuable, and collected by a re-cycler. And mattresses are no longer packed in cardboard; it is too expensive. In addition, if the commercial fishing fleet is in, grocery stores reserve all their large boxes for delivering food to the boats. It took me a day to source an adequate-sized box in Port Hardy. Next time I will phone ahead and ask the bike store to reserve one, and maybe even offer to pay.

North Island Forestry Centre (PI1)

Depending on your direction of travel, this is the last connection with the coast for a while, or the first. The centre is a joint venture of the forest companies operating in the area, and intended to acquaint the general public with their activities. In addition to housing exhibits and reference material, the centre coordinates a variety of forest tours with diverse themes which include log handling, railway rides, a fish hatchery, and an elk tracking program. This is a refreshing manner to learn more about a complex industry without the emotions and biases that often attend it.

The centre is also a convenient location to replenish water bottles.

Telegraph Cove (PI2)

Telegraph Cove, a village suspended above the water on stilts, is listed as having a year-round population of twelve. In the summer this balloons to thousands. Established before WWI, it was the northern terminus of a telgraph line that was strung tree-to-tree along the coast. Today it is a destination for sport fishermen and killer whale watchers, the latter in tour boats and kayaks.

Interest in killer whales is a recent phenomenon. Very little was known about them before the sixties. Considered too small to be of value to the whalers, they were never hunted commercially. However, feared by fishermen for their attacks on the salmon stock, seals, sea lions, and other whales they were frequently shot. In 1970 a concern for their numbers motivated extensive studies to gather the scientific data needed to manage them as a resource. In 1990 it was estimated that there are about four hundred BC killer whales, in about thirty pods. About half these migrate to Johnstone Strait in the summer to feed on the abundant salmon.

Robson Bight (PI3)

This is a popular destination for whale watching tours originating in Telegraph Cove. It is the location of the rubbing beach, a gravel bed in about four meters of water in which whales congregate to rub. First discovered in 1973 there is no record of a similar rendezvous anywhere else on our coast. The theory for this extraordinary behaviour is that rubbing against the gravel removes parasites.

Port McNeill (PI4)

The camping cyclist could be excused for dismissing Port McNeill as only a departure point for the ferry to Alert Bay and Sointula. This town of twenty-seven hundred has logging as a primary focus, and fishing a distant second. It demonstrates, at least to the casual visitor, little interest in playing the tourism or hospitality game. A recent study on North Island tourism identified as a constraint the Port McNeill "municipal government preference for developing forestry over tourism."

Rather than re-invent itself in the face of extensive and sometimes exaggerated criticism of logging, Port McNeill has opted to "redefine" itself. Gone is the image of the logger as the prince of the woods. Businesses now sport banners proclaiming Port McNeill "tree-farm country."

In spite of its apparent indifference to tourism, I have always been treated cordially here. Of interest to cyclists, the community has a downtown campground (Broughton Straight Campsite, Mine Road, 956-3224) from which one can explore the surrounding network of logging roads.

Quatse River Campground (CG1)

61 sites, washrooms, showers

I selected Quatse River knowing only that it was close to town, and I needed shelter from the rain. It was an excellent choice, although at first I didn't think I would be admitted. The ferry from Prince Rupert had just arrived and all sites were taken. When I explained that I was a cyclist and didn't require much space, the manager hesitantly suggested I examine the area beside the picnic shelter. If it was okay for me I could stay there. It was and I did, for two days. A small grassy glade on the edge of the river, surrounded by trees with a picnic shelter nearby, it was one of the most pleasant spots I had occupied all summer. And the manager was reluctant to charge me for it.

As an added treat the Quatse River Campground shares the premises of a fish hatchery which is open to visitors. Every year this hatchery releases six species of salmon, including millions of juvenile pink salmon, and trout into the Quatse and other nearby streams,

Port Hardy (PI5)

Port Hardy, population five thousand, could easily be down, but it isn't. For years its economic cornerstones have been mining, forestry, and fishing. Employment here was high, as were wages. The mine, an open pit copper mine (length 1.5 miles, width .75 miles, depth 1320 ft, maximum employment one thousand) was scheduled for closure at the end of 1995, and will be flooded with salt water from the nearby inlet. The forestry industry, always subject to cyclical fluctuations, continues to be beset by land-use issues. And the fishery, at least temporarily, has declined.

The town's response has been to capitalize on its outdoor appeal to visitors from around the world. Its already-considerable hiking, cycling and kayaking venues are being expanded even more. In addition the sport fishery, still healthy, has added other species like halibut, ling cod and snapper.

Port Hardy is a very hospitable town, if those who work at its businesses are an indication. I met many during my hunt for the elusive bike box, and was always treated with courtesy and concern. Several even interrupted their work to assist me. An example of this community's commitment to visitors is its Infocentre. When I visited it was open seven days a week, twelve hours a day.

I.V.'s Quartermaster Pub

6555 Hardy Bay Road (949-6922)

As indicated earlier, this is not neighbourhood-pub country. This pub is unique mainly because it exists. The service is fast and friendly, and portions generous.

It is located at the top of the goverment wharf, at which is moored some of the commercial fleet. A glance at which hints at the extent of the massive capital and human resource commitment to this industry, and its economic impact on the Island coastal communities.

Cape Scott Provincial Park (CG2) — a ride not taken

hiker/biker tenting at San Josef Bay

The weekend that I cycled to Port Hardy, Alison and my oldest daughter toured Cape Scott. Alison had wanted ("pestered" also fits here) to go there since shortly after we moved to the Island. The park is primarily a hiking venue with its most desirable campsites over twenty kilometres of muddy trail from the main entrance. Because of my bad knees it held little appeal to me. Consequently it never occurred to me to cycle there as part of my research on Hardy.

After viewing the photographs of Alison's trip, I wish I had. Its beauty, although more isolated, rivals that of the Long Beach unit at Pacific Rim National Park. There is camping for cyclists at San Josef Bay.

Cape Scott is reached on a sixty kilometre gravel-surfaced road from Port hardy. It rains here frequently.

More on bike boxes

Because this is the last chapter of my last book (Also my first book. Isn't English a bizarre language?), it presents a final opportunity for a humourous self-deprecating anecdote.

Before moving to the Island I was an executive with a national consulting firm, a position which I'd like to think required sound planning skills. The bike box which I finally sourced was at The Furniture Gallery, a downtown furniture and appliance store. The manager, Dugald MacMillan had gone to some lengths to locate one at a branch store and was having it sent over by truck. When after several hours it had not arrived, he offered to have it delivered to my campsite, some eight kilometres distant. That evening it was dropped off for me. I stored it in a

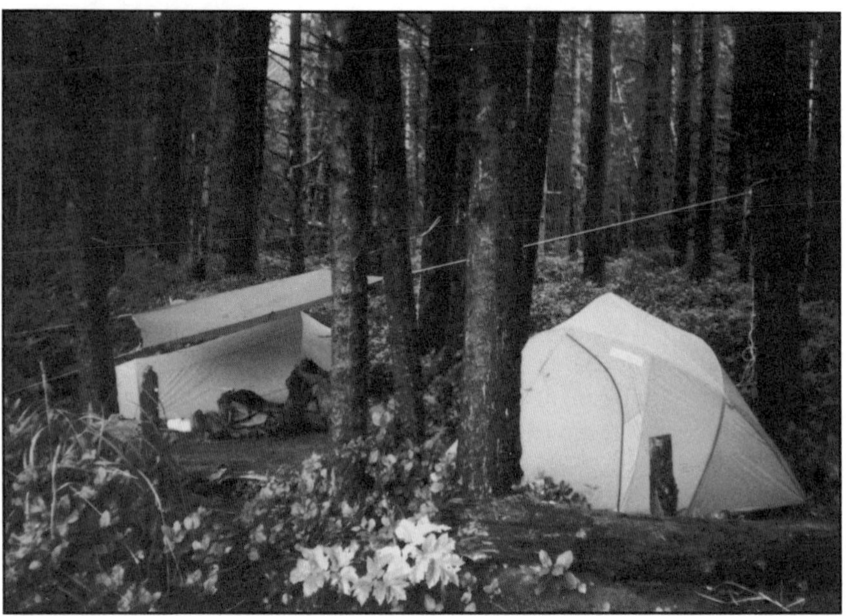

Port Hardy — San Josef Bay

nearby building for the night, content that I now had a bike box but suddenly concerned about my ability to haul it to the bus depot.

The trip there the next morning was an adventure, trying to carry this monstrous box under one arm, and steer a fully loaded bike. Every time a vehicle breezed by, the box behaved like a sail, trying to push me into situations that were potentially very painful. I made it, but here's the kicker. The Furniture Gallery is four doors down from the bus terminal, and the box could easily have been left for me there, had I only thought to ask. Living on the Island can do funny things to your head.

In closing, have I mentioned that I was thinking of writing a book on my cycling and camping experiences on Vancouver Island? Maybe even include a few pubs.

Postscript

We still haven't gone to Ireland. Early in the process of researching this book, Alison offered her help with photograhy, editing, research, and recollections of past adventures. We realized we were doing it together, and enjoying it.

Perhaps Ireland wasn't necessary. We were already sharing a dream.

Appendix I

Metric Conversion Table

Length

1 kilometre (km)	=	0.6214 miles	1 mile = 1.6093 km
1 metre (m)	=	1.0936 yards	1 yard (yd.) = 0.9144 m
1 centimetre (cm)	=	0.3937 inches	1 foot (ft.) = 0.3048 m
			1 inch (in.) = 2.54 cm

Volume

1 litre (l)	=	0.2200 Imp. gal.	1 Imperial gallon (gal.) = 4.5455 l
	=	(0.2642 US gal.)	(1 US gallon) = 3.7854 l
1 litre (l)	=	1.7599 Imp. pt.	1 Imperial pint (pt.) = 0.5682 l
		(2.1132 US pt.)	(1 US pint) = 0.4732 l

Area

1 hectare (ha)	=	2.4711 acres	1 acre = 0.4047 ha

Mass (Weight)

1 tonne (t)	=	1.1023 tons	1 ton = 0.9072 t
1 kilogram (kg)	=	2.2046 pounds	1 pound (lb.) = 0.4536 kg
1 gram (g)	=	0.0353 ounces	1 ounce (oz.) = 28.350 g

Temperature

100° Celsius (C)	=	212° Fahrenheit (F)
32°C	=	90°F
27°C	=	80°F
21°C	=	70°F
16°C	=	60°F
10°C	=	50°F
0°C	=	32°F

To convert °C to °F: multiply by 1.8 and add 32. To convert °F to °C: subtract 32 and divide by 1.8.

Appendix II

Distance Chart

	Campbell River	Courtenay	Duncan	Ladysmith	Lake Cowichan	Nanaimo	Parksville	Port Alberni	Port Hardy	Port McNeill	Port Renfrew	Qualicum Beach	Sidney	Sooke	Tofino	Ucluelet
Campbell River																
Courtenay	45															
Duncan	204	159														
Ladysmith	176	131	28													
Lake Cowichan	226	182	30	51												
Nanaimo	153	108	51	23	73											
Parksville	117	73	87	58	109	36										
Port Alberni	151	106	135	107	157	84	50									
Port Hardy	238	282	441	413	464	391	355	389								
Port McNeill	198	243	402	374	425	352	316	350	44							
Port Renfrew	349	304	145	173	175	196	232	280	586	547						
Qualicum Beach	107	62	97	69	120	47	11	45	344	305	242					
Sidney	284	239	80	108	110	131	167	215	522	483	127	178				
Sooke	279	234	75	103	105	126	162	210	517	478	70	172	57			
Tofino	273	228	256	228	279	206	171	122	510	471	401	166	337	331		
Ucluelet	248	203	231	203	253	180	146	96	485	446	376	141	311	306	42	
Victoria	264	219	60	88	90	111	147	195	502	463	107	158	26	37	316	291

Distances shown are in kilometres. 1 kilometre = 0.6214 miles.

APPENDIX III

Travel Infocentres

British Columbia Infocentres are hosted by knowledgeable staff and well stocked with local and regional information, most of which is free. The provincial government also maintains a tourism home page on the Internet at: *http://www.gov.bc.ca/tourism/tourism.html.* In addition, a growing number of individual communities are maintaining their own Internet sites. At this writing most of these were still new and sparse in content, but as familiarity with the information highway increases, they are expected to become more comprehensive.

- • all British Columbia area codes are currently (604). However to accommodate our population growth additional codes are planned.
- •• seasonal operation only.

Location	Address	Phone•	Fax•
Alert Bay	116 Fir Street Box 28 Alert Bay, BC V0N 1A0	974-5213	974-5470
Campbell River	1235 Shopper's Row Box 400 Campbell River, BC V9W 5B6	287-4636	286-6490
Chemainus••	9758 Chemainus Road Box 575 Chemainus, BC V0R 1K0	246-4701	246-3251
Colwood/Langford	697 Goldstream Avenue Victoria, BC V9B 2X2	478-1130	478-1584
Courtenay/ Comox Valley	2040 Cliffe Avenue Courtenay, BC V9N 2L3	334-3234	334-4908
Crofton••	1507 Joan Avenue Box 128 Crofton, BC V0R 1R0	246-2456	246-2287
Cumberland••	PO Box 74 Cumberland, BC V0R 1S0	336-8313	336-2455
Duncan-Cowichan	381 Trans-Canada Hwy. Duncan, BC V9L 3R5	746-4636	746-8222
Lake Cowichan••	125C South Shore Rd. Box 824 Lake Cowichan, BC V0R 2G0	749-3244	749-3900

Nanaimo	256 Bryden Street Nanaimo, BC V9S 1A8	754-8474 1-800-663-7337	754-6468
Parksville	1275 East Island Hwy. Box 99 Parksville, BC V9P 2G3	248-3613	248-5210
Port Alberni	2533 Redford Street RR2, Site 215, Comp 10 Port Alberni, BC V9Y 7L6	724-6535	724-6560
Port Hardy	7250 Market Street Box 249 Port Hardy, BC V0N 2P0	949-7622	949-6653
Port McNeill	Beach Drive Box 129 Port McNeill, BC V0N 2R0	956-3131	956-4977
Powell River	4690 Marine Avenue Powell River, BC V8A 2L1	485-4701	485-2822
Qualicum Beach	2711 West Island Hwy. Qualicum Beach, BC V9K 2C4	752-9532	752-2923
Saanich Peninsula	10382 Patricia Bay Hwy. Box 2014 Sidney, BC V8L 3S3	656-0525	656-7102
Salt Spring Island	121 Lower Ganges Road Box 111 Ganges, BC V0S 1E0	537-5252	537-4276
Sooke	2070 Phillips Road Box 774 Sooke, BC V0S 1N0	642-6351	642-7089
Tofino••	380 Campbell St. Box 476 Tofino, BC V0R 2Z0	725-3414	725-3296
Ucluelet	227 Main Street Box 428 Ucluelet, BC V0R 3A0	726-4641	726-4611
Victoria	812 Wharf Street Victoria, BC V8W 1T3	382-2127	382-6539

Bibliography

Barnard, John L. *Victoria, British Columbia.* John L. Barnard Photographer, Victoria, BC.

Bowes, Dan. *Area Profile, Capital Regional District.* Report prepared for Victoria CEC, 1993.

Burton, Teresa. *Hiking Through History.* Port Renfrew Community Association, 1993.

Comox Valley Community Profile, The. Report prepared by the Comox Valey Chamber of Commerce, 1994.

Homan, Brian. *Port Alberni Community Profile.* Report prepared for Port Alberni CEC, 1994.

Lillard, Charles. *Discover Nanaimo.* The Greater Nanaimo Chamber of Commerce, Nanaimo, BC, 1992.

Lynden, Lauren. *Nanaimo Canada Employment Centre Community Profile.* Report prepared for Nanaimo CEC, 1994.

McVeigh Consulting. *North Island Tourism Information Compilation and Community Consultations.* Study prepared for the Ministry of Small Business, Tourism and Culture, *1995.*

Mussio, Russel and Wesley. *Backroad and Outdoor Recreation Mapbook.* Mussio Ventures Ltd., Surrey, BC, 1994.

Obee, Bruce. *The Gulf Islands Explorer.* Whitecap Books, North Vancouver, BC, 1981.

Priest, Simon. *Bicycling Vancouver Island and the Gulf Islands.* Douglas and McIntyre, Vancouver, BC, 1984.

Snowden, Mary Ann. *Island Paddling.* Orca Book Publishers, Victoria, BC, 1990.

Turner, Robert D. *Logging by Rail.* Sono Nis Press, Victoria, BC, 1990.

Wolferstan, Bill. *Cruising Guide to British Columbia Vol. 1, Gulf Islands and Vancouver Island from Sooke to Courtenay*, Whitecap Books, Vancouver/Toronto, 1987.

Wolferstan, Bill. *Cruising Guide to British Columbia Vol. 2, Desolation Sound and the Discovery Islands.* Whitecap Books, Vancouver/Toronto, 1989.

Zdancewicz, E.J. *Campbell River and North Vancouver Island Labour Market Review.* Report prepared for Campbell River CEC, 1995.

A

Alberni Inlet, 116
Alert Bay, 161
Amphitrite Point, 120
Arlington Inn, 109
Assembly Docks, 101

B

Bald Eagle Campsite, 93
Bamberton Provincial Park, 72
Bamberton Site, 72
Bamfield, 84
Baynes Sound, 128
Bazan Bay, 46
BC Ferries, 9, 44, 50, 66, 101, 114, 145
BC Forestry Museum, 91
Beach Country, 123
Beacon Hill Park, 59
Bears, 40, 113, 154
Beaver Cove, 160
Beaver Point, 65
Bere Point Regional Park, 161, 163, 166
Big Qualicum River Fish Hatchery, 127
Big Tree Creek Fish Hatchery, 157
Bilge Pub, 166
Black Bear Pub, 99, 103
Blue Grouse Vineyards, 73
Blue Heron Inn, 122
Boat Harbour, 105
Boomerang Lake, 113
Botanical Beach Provincial Park, 84
Bowser, 125
Bradsdadsland Waterfront Camping, 131, 133, 136
Brannen Lake Campsites, 99, 103
Brass Bell Pub, 92
Brentwood Bay, 46
Broughton Strait, 169
Buckley Bay, 131, 137
Buttle Lake, 149

C

Cameron Lake, 107, 109
Campbell River, 8, 33, 129, 147, 150, 154
Campbellton, 151
Campgrounds, 38, 39, 40
Camping, 24, 25, 27
Canadian air force base, 138
Canadian Forest Products Ltd., 159
Cape Mudge, 152, 153
Cape Scott Provincial Park, 173
Carmannah Pacific Park, 80
Cathedral Grove, 107, 111
Central Island, 8
Chemainus, 81, 89, 93
Chemainus mill, 82
Cherry Point, 76
Clayoquot Sound, 122
Clothing, 20, 21, 31, 32
CNR, 81
Cobble Hill, 69, 73, 74
Cobblestone Inn, 73
Cock and Bull, 59
Comox, 129, 137, 138, 140, 142, 147
Comox air force base, 143
Comox Valley, 123, 133, 138, 142, 147
Cooking, 26, 30
Coombs, 107, 109, 110, 113
Coral Reef, 158
Cormorant Island, 161, 165, 170
cougars, 40, 113
Courtenay, 33, 123, 125, 138, 140, 141, 142, 147
Courtenay and District Museum, 142
Cowichan Bay, 69, 81
Cowichan Lake, 77, 79, 83, 86
Cowichan River, 81
Cowichan River Railway Beds, 81
Cowichan Valley, 47, 71, 82
Cowichan Valley Wine Road, 69
Crofton, 47, 63, 81, 87, 89
Crofton Bay, 92
Crofton Hotel, 92
Crow and Gate, 105
Cumberland, 129, 138, 140, 141
Cumberland Museum, 141

D

Deep Bay, 137
Deer Creek Park Public Campground, 112
Denman Island, 125, 128, 131, 133, 138
Desolation Sound, 163
Dinghy Dock Pub, 101
Discovery Channel, 150
Discovery Passage, 147, 152
Discovery Pier, 151
Dominion Astrophysical Observatory, 49
Drumbeg Park, 104

Dry Creek Park, 109
Duncan, 33, 69, 71, 73, 74, 77, 81, 82, 87, 89, 90

E

Eagle's Nest Marine Pub, 120
Elk Falls Provincial Park, 147, 149, 151
Elk Falls Pulp and Paper Mill, 157
Elk Lake, 46
Empress Hotel, 58
Esquimalt, 52, 54, 55, 57, 81

F

Fairy Lake, 84
Fanny Bay, 129, 137
Fanny Bay Inn, 128
Fernwood, 68
Fillongley Provincial Park, 133, 134
First aid, 33, 34
Fish farms, 126
Fisherboy Campground, 157, 158
Ford's Cove, 131, 133
Forestry industry, 11, 39
Frontiersman Pub, 110
Fulford Harbour, 47, 63, 67, 68
Fulford Harbour Inn, 63, 65

G

Gabriola Island, 104
Galloping Goose Regional Trail, 60
Ganges, 61, 63, 64, 65, 68
General Hill, 151, 152
Genoa Bay, 87, 92
Glenora, 81
Gold River, 147, 151
Goldstream Provincial Park, 54, 55, 56
Goodwin, Ginger, 142
Gordon Bay Provincial Park, 77, 79
Gordon River, 83, 86
Greater Victoria Cycling Coalition, 54
Green Point, 116, 118, 121
Griffin Pub, 141, 144
Gulf Islands, 4, 9, 47, 50, 64, 67, 76, 91, 106

H

Hackson Emu Farm, 143
Handlebars, 13, 17, 33
Helliwell Provincial Park, 136
Helmets, 21
Hemer Park, 105
Heriot Bay Inn, 153
Hillcrest, 83
Hornby Island, 125, 131, 133, 134, 138
Hornby Island Co-op, 136
Hornby Island Resort, 135
Horne Lake, 127, 129
Horne Lake Caves Provincial Park, 130
Horne Lake Family Campground, 130
Horseshoe Bay, 146
Horseshoe Bay Inn, 94
Hump, The, 107, 109, 111

I

I.V. Quatermaster Pub, 173
Inland Lake, 146
Inner Harbour, 57
Island Highway, 87, 89, 96, 101, 123, 147, 152, 154

J

Jingle Pot Pub, 99, 104
John Hart Dam, 149, 152

K

Kelsey Bay, 157, 158
Kin Beach Campsite, 140, 144
Kingfisher Oceanside Inn, 129, 140
Kwagiulth First Nations Museum, 153

L

Lady Rose, 116, 118, 119
Ladysmith, 81, 87, 89, 94, 95
Ladysmith Inn, 95
Lake Cowichan, 77, 80, 81, 82
Langdale, 146
Lantzville, 109
Lantzville Village Pub, 99, 103
Leechtown, 60
Little Qualicum Falls Provincial Park, 109, 110, 111
Little Qualicum River, 111
Little River, 141, 145
Living Forest Oceanside Campground, 99, 100
Lizard Lake, 84
Log Train Trail, 114, 130
Logging, 77, 80, 82, 154, 159
Logging roads, 5, 79, 83, 112, 113
Long Beach, 120, 121
Long Harbour, 67
Lopez Island, 50
Lorne Hotel, 143

M

M.V. *Lady Rose*, 116, 118, 119
Ma Miller's Inn, 56
MacMillan Bloedel Ltd., 112, 159
Malahat Drive, 7, 47, 63, 76
Malcolm Island, 161, 165, 170
Maple Bay, 91
McDonald Provincial Park, 46, 47, 48, 49
Merridale Cider Works, 72
Merville, 147
Mill Bay, 47, 69, 71, 72
Mills, 80, 81, 87, 89, 90, 128, 145
Miracle Beach Provincial Park, 149, 150
Moddle, David, 26, 27, 65, 105, 113
Mouat Provincial Park, 63, 65, 68
Mount Arrowsmith, 113
Mount Benson, 106
Mount Geoffrey, 137
Mount Maxwell Provincial Park, 67
Mount Washington, 144
Mud Bay, 129

N

Nanaimo, 33, 47, 81, 87, 96, 98, 99, 107, 129, 170
Nanaimo Harbour, 100
Nanaimo Lakes, 106
Nanoose, 107, 109
Native Heritage Centre, 91
Newcastle Island Provincial Park, 102
Nimpkish Valley, 154, 160
Nimpkish Burial Grounds, 164
Nimpkish Camp, 169
Nimpkish Hotel and Pub, 165
Nimpkish Lake, 169
North Cowichan, 87, 90
North Island, 8
North Island Forestry Centre, 170
Northwest Bay, 112, 114

O

Oak Bay, 52, 54
Oceanview Campsite, 161, 163, 164
Odometer, 18
Orcas Island, 50
Osborne Bay Resort, 92
Outback Oven, 28, 31
Oysters, 128

P

Pacific Grey Whales, 120
Pacific Rim National Park, 38, 116, 120
Page's Resort and Marina, 105
Panniers, 16, 18
Parksville, 123, 125
Personal safety, 10
Pipers Lagoon Park, 102
Port Alberni, 107, 111, 129
Port Augusta, 142
Port Hardy, 8, 167, 169, 172
Port McNeill, 154, 159, 161, 167, 169, 171
Port Renfrew, 6, 54, 79, 83, 84
Port Renfrew Hotel, 85
Port Renfrew Marina & Campground, 84, 85
Potlatches, 164
Powell River, 145
Prairie Inn, 49
Prince Rupert, 169
Private campgrounds, 39
Protection Island, 101
Provincial Legislature, 58
Provincial parks, 38, 39
Pubs, 30, 35, 36, 37

Q

Quadra Island, 147, 149, 152, 153
Qualicum Beach, 125, 129
Quathiaski Cove, 152
Quatse River Campground, 170, 172
Queen Charlotte Strait, 169
Quinsam Hotel, 151

R

Rail's End Pub, 82
Railway bed, 77
Rathtrevor Beach Provincial Park, 125, 127
Rebecca Spit Provincial Park, 153
Rhododendron Lake, 113
Ripple Rock, 157
Riverside Inn, 86
Roberts Lake, 156
Robson Bight, 164, 171
Rocking Horse Pub, 114
Roy, Colleen, 24
Roy Vickers' Eagle Aerie Gallery, 122
Royal BC Museum, 57
Royal Coachman Pub, 149, 151
Ruckle Provincial Park, 61, 63, 65, 66

S
Saanich, 52
Saanich Peninsula, 44, 51, 76
Salmon Point Marine Pub, 149, 150
Saltair Pub, 94
Salt Spring Island, 61, 63, 64, 67, 93
San Juan Islands, 50, 66
San Juan Valley, 84
Sayward, 4, 154, 156, 157, 158
Seats, 14, 17, 19
Security, 37
Seymour Narrows Lookout, 157
Shack Islands, 102
Shady Rest, 127
Shawnigan Lake, 76
Shelter Point Park, 146
Sidney, 44, 46, 48, 49, 50, 51
Silva Bay Pub, 105
Skutz Falls, 81
Sointula, 161
Sooke Potholes Provincial Park, 60
Sooke River, 60
South Island, 7, 44
Spit Trail, 136
Spokes, 19, 23
Stamp Falls Provincial Park, 115
Stonehouse Pub, 48
Stoves, 27, 31, 33
Stowell Lake, 67
Strait of Georgia, 123, 125, 144, 145, 147, 150
Sunshine Coast, 145, 146
Swartz Bay, 44, 46, 47, 48, 63, 65

T
Telegraph Cove, 167, 170, 171
Tents, 25
Texada Island, 145, 146
Thatch Pub, 134
The Hump, 107, 109, 111
Thetis Island, 93
Thetis Lake, 54
Tires, 15, 19, 22
Tofino, 116, 118, 121
Tool kit, 18, 20
Trailhead Campsite, 84, 85
Travel Infocentres, 10, 176, 177
Tribune Bay, 133
Tribune Bay Provincial Park, 133, 135
Tsawwassen, 47
Tuck, Andrew, 12, 13
Tudor House Pub, 57
Tyee Club, 150
Tyee Spit, 151

U
Ucluelet, 116, 118, 119
U'mista Cultural Centre, 164
Union Bay, 129
Uplands, 54

V
Vancouver Island, 3, 4, 5, 6, 7, 35
Vancouver Island Brewery, 58, 59
Venturi-Schulze Vineyards, 74
Vesuvius, 47, 63, 67, 92
Vesuvius Inn, 64
Victoria, 8, 33, 44, 46, 47, 52, 54, 55, 56, 87
View Royal, 60
Vignetti Zanatta, 74

W
Washington State Ferries, 50, 51
Water bottles, 16, 37
Water filter, 29
West Coast Trail, 84, 85, 120
Whaling Station Bay, 136
White Hart Pub, 105
Woss, 159
Woss Camp, 154, 160
Woss Lake Campground, 160

Y
Yellow Point, 105
Youbou, 77, 86